THE MEMORIALISTS

An Antebellum History of
Alleghany, Craig, and
Monroe Counties
of
Western Virginia

1812~1860

David Scott Turk

HERITAGE BOOKS
2011

HERITAGE BOOKS
AN IMPRINT OF HERITAGE BOOKS, INC.

Books, CDs, and more—Worldwide

For our listing of thousands of titles see our website at
www.HeritageBooks.com

Published 2011 by
HERITAGE BOOKS, INC.
Publishing Division
100 Railroad Ave. #104
Westminster, Maryland 21157

Copyright © 1997 David Scott Turk

Other Heritage Books by the author:

A Family's Path in America: The Lees and Their Continuing Legacy

Give My Kind Regards to the Ladies: The Life of Littleton Quinton Washington

The Memorialists: An Antebellum History of Alleghany, Craig, and Monroe Counties of Western Virginia, 1812-60

The Union Hole: Unionist Activity and Local Conflict in Western Virginia

All rights reserved. No part of this book may be reproduced or transmitted in any form or by any means, electronic or mechanical, including photocopying, recording or by any information storage and retrieval system without written permission from the author, except for the inclusion of brief quotations in a review.

International Standard Book Numbers
Paperbound: 978-0-7884-0687-4
Clothbound: 978-0-7884-8895-5

Contents

Chapter 1.	Emerging From Wilderness: Before 1820	1
Chapter 2.	The Sweet Springs Courthouse, the Cases and Its People	9
Chapter 3.	Bottles and Politics: Temperance and Political Movements 1820-1860	26
Chapter 4.	New Gates: The Emergence of Toll Roads and Businesses 1820-1860	50
Chapter 5.	The Farmer-Soldier Communities in Wartime: 1812-15 and 1845-48	74
Chapter 6.	The Religious Community	80
Chapter 7.	Educating the Populace	88
Family Sketches of the Region		93
Appendix A. List of Fines - 108th Virginia Militia, 1814		107
Appendix B. Roll of U. S. Volunteers		113

Illustrations

1. Map of the Potts Creek Valley, ca. 1847.   viii
From Legislative Petitions. Courtesy: VA State Library.
Photograph by Glenn Vogel.

2. Political Steel Engraving (c. 1853) showing   facing 26
President Franklin Pierce surrounded by past
Presidents. Author's Collections.

3. Legislative Petition: This one was against the   facing 42
formation of Craig County. Many opposed the
new county due to the distance or costs of supporting
public buildings. Courtesy: VA State Library.
Photograph by Glenn Vogel.

4. Augustus A. Chapman, U. S. Senator and local   facing 49
businessman. (1803-1876). Courtesy:
Peggy Thompson Steele.

5. Fulton Stoneware. Courtesy: Helen Baker.   facing 68
Photograph by Glenn Vogel.

Acknowledgments

As with any sizeable project, there are more people to thank than possible to list. My wife Janet and son Ryan, now two years old, allowed the research time and encouragement. Ryan assisted by drawing some appropriate squiggles on my initial draft and making me chase him for my ink pen. Thanks must go to the patient librarians and archivists at the Fairfax Library Virginia Room, the Virginia State Library, Duke University Special Collections, and Colson Hall at the University of West Virginia. Others to be thanked are Nora Martin, Stewart Bostic, Sylvia Echols, Louise Collins Perkins, Helen Humphries, Leonard Jamison, Lucy Hurst, Norma Paxton Harris, Watson Smith, and Pullen Sizer. Inspiration from my academic guides, particularly George Mason University Professors Jane Turner Censer, Peter Henriques, Ted McCord, and Ken Bolling, along with historian Ted Calhoun, were the primary instructors that gave me the crucial education I needed to get this far. Special inspiration also go to friends: the Greg Blank family; my brother-in-law Glenn Vogel, a New Jersey historian in his own right; Anthony Corbitt; Mark Kline; and my entire family. There are numerous unnamed others to thank, and their contributions are as important to me.

To the late Charles "Rip" Gulbrandson: Your good humor and hard work will always be an influence on me.

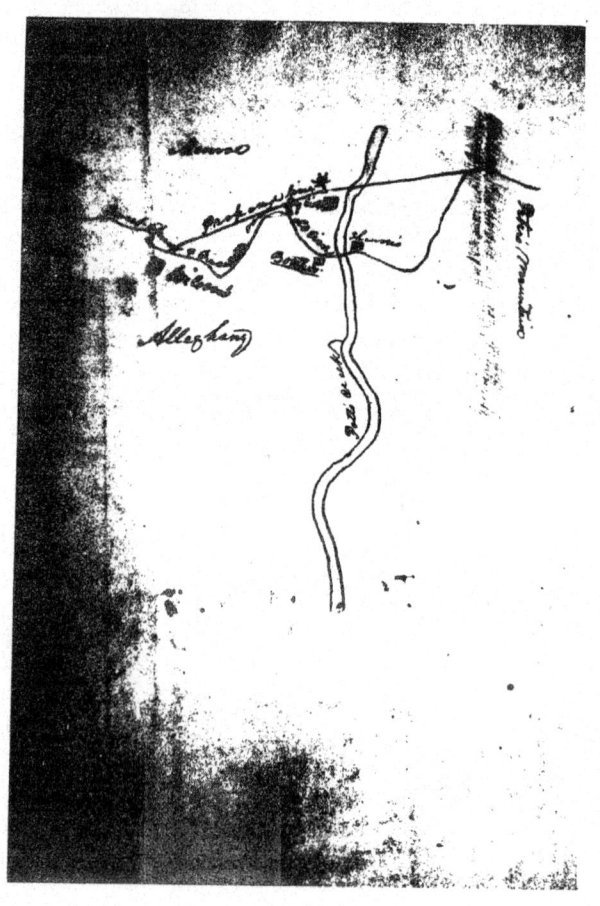

Map of the Potts Creek Valley, ca. 1847. From Legislative Petitions.
Courtesy: VA State Library. Photograph by Glenn Vogel.

December 1994

My studies of western Virginia transported me to a fascinating time of carriages, turnpikes, temperance societies and political awakening. To understand the American Civil War, a good study of what caused it is required. Actually, western Virginia started to break away from the eastern portion of the state a lot earlier than the 1850s. The internal rift over the building of turnpikes, canals and railroads ensured bitterness over any slavery issue. The western farmers felt that bitterness when Henry Clay's American System failed in their state. They plodded through with a secondary road system until turnpikes vastly expanded in the mid-1840s. The James River and Kanawha Canal was Virginia tradition that interested many great men and also kept this part of Virginia from advanced improvements. On the local level, legislative petitions and court records reveal entrepreneurs and an emerging business elite in forming turnpike companies and tavern ownership. The business elite was the political elite in most cases. The same records also indicated that the mountain farmer was an aware and active lobbying force on many issues such as turnpike improvement, voting precincts and the formation of counties.

Politics became a reality in western Virginia. With the rise of Andrew Jackson and the frontier President, mountain farmers felt represented by one of their own. Henry Clay and his Whig Party was respected by the business class. With business and politics came the reform movements like the idea of organized temperance societies. Although the religious revivals in this area did much to bring movements about or even to help rationalize their need, business drove the framework.

Business was politics. Business was taverns and springs, ironworks and roads. The Potts' Creek Valley in Alleghany and Monroe Counties had all of these industries. The industries and the men who emerged as the community leaders turned what was a wild frontier into an integral part of American society. It became fashionable to vacation at the Virginia springs and dine at Colonel John Crow's tavern. Leisure was business here. With the notable exception of the iron industry, most of the growth in business came around the weary vacationer or the state legislature.

However, this book is not just about business. It's about how people dealt with each other in social situations, such as a simple land dispute, drinking, the vote or spousal abuse. It gives a fuller picture of who was working behind those lush landscapes of the springs. The famous corresponded with the not-so-famous. Perhaps it points out why the people of western Virginia are so enlightened. As I like to say, they are the "last of the genteel Virginians."

DT

Chapter 1.-Emerging From Wilderness

In 1812, the Potts Creek Valley in western Virginia was a quiet and wild place. Wild game abounded and the forests were full. Settlers were few. Those settler who had come west had done so primarily in hopes of a more prosperous life which had been denied in eastern Virginia. Some had come for the privacy of more open spaces. Of course, many families had already settled in the area. In Sweet Springs, where increasing numbers of families and individuals were visiting either to vacation or to recover from illness, the Lewis family lived at a wilderness residence called the Wigwam.[1]

The earliest settlers had braved Indian incursions and the hard life of a pioneer. By 1812 the indigenous Indians were residing elsewhere. Modern comforts were only slowly arriving. The roads were rough in the mountains. Only the mineral springs and vacation spas remained as a source of economic prosperity.

Ann & William Royall

There were those who had come to live in those spacious surroundings of mountain life. Major William Royall was such a man. The son of the landowner aristocracy in eastern Virginia, he had served as a state legislator during the Revolutionary War. When British Colonel Banistre Tarleton raided the Virginia piedmont, the terrified delegates to the legislature fled westward over the Blue Ridge Mountains to Staunton. When rumors followed that Tarleton's cavalry was pursuing them, some of the delegates fled Staunton. Royall and some of the western commoners stayed to fight but the anticipated invasion never took place. Major Royall demonstrated that he preferred the company of the much maligned westerner to the eastern Virginians with whom he had grown up.[2]

Royall acquired several tracts of wilderness land. One plot constituted 165 acres on Potts Creek, and another was situated along the Greenbrier River. Royall settled into his new home on the slopes of Peter's Mountain. Once there, the cultured major set up his library and proceeded to have a profound intellectual influence on his fellow settlers.[3]

The major was visited by many of the local frontiersmen, as well as relatives and distinguished guests. Potts Creek Valley farmers James Linton and James Wiley were frequent visitors. Tavernkeep John Shawver and his relative Christopher were known to have visited the major. Through their acquaintance with the aristocratic and intellectual Major Royall, the farmers and craftsmen unwittingly heightened their own sense of refinement. Behind their rough facades, they became enlightened. Matthew Dunbar, for instance, a young local lawyer who studied in the major's personal library, eventually became a famous state jurist.[4]

Major Royall had married Anne Newport in 1797. Anne was a Pennsylvania native whose mother was a servant in the Lewis family household at the Wigwam. The marriage was later questioned during a court case brought about by a relative contesting the major's will. Despite her later troubles, Anne's published accounts of her later sojourns were to prove invaluable to a less mobile public in *Letters from Alabama* and *Manners & Customs in the United States*, where she provided much description of the country.[5]

When the major died in late 1812, his widow's relationships with the surrounding Potts Creek Valley farmers deteriorated. John Lewis, the son of William Lewis, was less than enthusiastic about Anne and her relations with the local farmers. Unfortunately for her, John Lewis wielded great influence. He lent money to many of the local farmers to purchase land and implements. Without the respected influence of the major, Anne could not improve relations with the new master of the Sweet Springs spa and would eventually leave Peter's Mountain to embark on a distinguished career.[6]

The Lewis Influence

By 1812, the Lewis Family was already enjoying the fruits of prosperity in the Potts Creek Valley. John's Uncle, General Andrew Lewis, had been a hero in both Dunmore's War against the Indians in 1774 and the Revolutionary War. Andrew and his brother Charles had fought local Indians in the area led by Chief Cornstalk during the earlier conflict. The successful action at Point Pleasant, near the Ohio River, opened the Potts Creek Valley and the surrounding lands to safer habitation. The family would be memorialized in the renaming of Fort Savannah as Lewisburg.[7]

John Lewis himself was a Revolutionary soldier of some stature. He was mentioned by President Andrew Jackson in 1832 during the South Carolina secession crisis. Jackson stated that if he had more men like the late Lewis, he could punish the actions of politicians John C. Calhoun and Henry Clay together.[8]

John's father William was a pariah of local politics in the region. Before his death in 1811, William was running both a successful vacation resort and maintaining public facilities. The district court was held at the Sweet Springs until 1807. The Potts Creek Valley attracted many people-especially learned lawyers-who wished to reside near the court. After the court moved on, the local populace still silently acknowledged the legitimacy of holding various meetings to settle disputes at Sweet Springs. William Lewis' plans served to ensure the survival of Sweet Springs and its surroundings for some time.[9]

John Lewis continued to build on his father's dream of a resort-centered community, which he inherited in his mid-30s. Although the court never returned to the Springs after 1807, the mineral spa baths flourished. People traveled to Sweet Springs across the mountain terrain from all regions to convalesce or rest. Lewis' financial support was smart politics as well as confirming status as local patron. By lending money to rising farmers as landowners, they would in turn assist him by taking care of flourishing farm lands. The money fostered industry, productivity and resulted in more and more tilled fields, which led to transportation improvements in order to get produce to the eastern market. The mountain farmers became Lewis' allies in their common cause. When John Lewis died in 1823, he was unaware of how much he had transformed the surrounding area.[10]

Covington

From the hollows and valleys adjacent to Sweet Springs, other individuals came forward with new ideas of settlement and industry. Snake Run was described vividly by former Secretary of War James McHenry for its natural wonders and potential monetary means. Hugh Paul Taylor, a lawyer and civil engineer who resided at Lewisburg, took an interest in internal improvements in the region. John Pitzer and Dr. James Merry settled near an area called Mouth of Dunlap, located at the entrance to Dunlap Creek, another tributary near Potts Creek. Pitzer's store, which he had operated since about 1798, became a frontier outpost for dry goods and a place for ready credit, according to historian Harry Walton. Soon the town of Covington was formed on land sold to by George Pence to Merry for $3,000 in October 1817. The first plat map of the town was drawn up the following year, and the first town lots were sold at auction in August 1818.[12]

The town of Covington grew in the expectation that the James River and Kanawha Canal would reach and extend beyond the town. Virginia Governor John Tyler put forth this plan in his 1826 message to the House of Delegates.

> The necessity and propriety, then, of completing the improvement by rendering navigable the Jackson's River from Covington, and improving the navigation of James River, and thereby furnishing the intermediate link between the two extremes, must be entirely obvious.[13]

It never really happened. The rugged mountains proved formidable enough to halt canal construction just east of the town. A railroad was proposed to cover the remaining distance to the Greenbrier River. A survey of that river revealed numerous rocks and unexpected rapids that would impede construction efforts. Still, the residents of Covington and the Potts Creek Valley never gave up trying to improve their finances and market access. In time, the James River Company proved to be the enemy, not the friend, for these goals. Sectional and political tensions wracked the Company and kept it from meeting its original goals.[14]

Covington suffered growing pains. Although it was sufficiently large to be a town by 1819, it had to be incorporated twice. It did so the first time in 1833, but lost its status six years later. In 1840 it once again incorporated. Growth was slow. In 1855, 43 houses lined two primary streets, but surrounding areas had grown faster; an Act of Assembly of January 5, 1822, brought Alleghany County into existence.[15]

Some of the local businesses depended not on the expansion of canal, but rather on turnpike improvement and surface travel. Irishman Dennis Callaghan bought a tavern house on the road west, and his lodgings and good humor won space in Anne Royall's writings. Sam Houston's father was noted to have died at his inn. Of course, Callaghan was not alone in the enterprise of a tavern commercial center. Closer to Sweet Springs was Colonel John Crow's tavern, John Stringer set up shop close to the springs, and John Shawver's tavern lay east of Peter's Mountain.[16]

The ironworks appeared in the 1820's. John Jordan and John Irvine built the Lucy Selina furnace. They found a rich supply of iron ore in Potts Creek Valley and many years later, the place called Jordan Mines would still produce ore. The ore found in the antebellum period served as an important source of local income. Most of the labor was provided by slaves, and local citizens benefited from the increased value of their ore-laden lands.[17]

Farmers began to understand the value of political organization to achieve common goals. As Business grew, political organization followed. In the early 1800's, western Virginia was not much of a political force. In 1812, most individuals were fellow admirers of Virginians Thomas Jefferson, George Washington, or James Madison.

On a frontier where people simply tried to survive, formal politics was not a high priority.

The farmers of Potts Creek Valley had to travel over twenty mountainous miles to Fincastle, the seat of Botetourt County, to get a copy of the newspaper. Alleghany County did not exist as a separate political and geographic entity until 1822, and much of the Potts Creek Valley and surrounding terrain fell within the borders of Greenbrier or Botetourt Counties. The settlers were more closely rooted to local politics. In 1812, name recognition meant more than anything else and local names like Lewis or Stuart was practically assured office if one was running for one. But as economies developed and life grew more complicated, so did the politics.[18]

The social problems of complicated lives inevitably emerged. Drinking was always prevalent on the cold mountain evenings. At times excessive consumption led to broken homes and the loosening of economic and social ties. Although temperance proliferated among evangelical Protestants, no organized anti-alcohol group existed until the Sons of Temperance reached Covington in the late 1840's. It took much organization and discipline that took on a parade atmosphere. However, the attempts were eventually effective.[19]

In addition, many religious revivals were attended by these same settlers. Methodist camp meetings in the Potts Creek Valley and the vicinity were examples of some of the most influential regional religious activity. Bishop Francis Asbury personally stayed at Potts Creek. Itinerant preachers such as Joseph Pennell and Lorenzo Dow developed large followings. The influence of German Baptist and proponents of a fundamental Christianity that spread rapidly over the region. The Presbyterians were influential, particularly in the late

1780s and 1790s, before many other denominations were established. They continued to flourish under such active preachers as John McElhenney and Samuel R. Houston. Their teachings also converted some of their followers into sobriety.[20]

Sobriety and military strength were sources of community pride for many western Virginians. When the War of 1812 brought the new country into war, the men of Alleghany, Botetourt, and Monroe Counties joined local militia and fought the British. One notable unit from the area had the most common service in the war. Many never saw action, but participated in guard duty along the Virginia coast. Captain Andrew Nickell's company of the 4th Virginia Militia spent most of their service on guard duty on a disease-infested island in the Chesapeake Bay. The distance minimized the war's local impact. The Mexican War brought more uniformity to it's force, combining men of different areas into one unit. The community efforts were still there, but not in its traditional fashion.[21]

Tradition was once a necessity for the mountain farmer. Communities before 1820 needed the family and community ties to survive. By 1860, many of these traditional ties were challenged or broken by technological improvement and conflicting loyalty. The social hierarchy was shattered by the influence of interstate commerce and fast news distribution. The military contributions turned away from traditional local units. Religion went beyond dogma and observance, and entered the areas of social action, such as working toward temperance. Temperance became part-religion, part politics. With the knowledge of influence, the local populace wanted to increase their social and political influence on the state and the nation as a whole; the results were mixed.

Chapter 2. The Sweet Springs Courthouse: The Cases and the People

The Community-Town and Gathering Place

The courthouse was the focal point in the lives of many western Virginians. It was a place to discuss daily happenings, see elected officials, and resolve grievances. Commerce naturally drew to the courthouse. Given the correct direction, a full community could grow from the social centerpiece.

William Lewis was astute enough to recognize the attraction to the courthouse. From 1795 to 1807, Sweet Springs boasted a district court and jail that drew cases from Botetourt, Greenbrier, Kanawha, and Montgomery Counties. He also recognized the qualities of the water resources on his acreage. The sulfuric content of the spring water could easily draw many visitors from far places. In 1792, Lewis completed his first lodging house. Lewis' original plan had been to create a complete community to be named Fontville. He hoped for an all-inclusive community that grew from the benefits of spring water and a legal center.[1]

The concept of Fontville was damaged by Lewis himself. One of the dangers of mixing politics with business was that the former took precedence over the latter. It also allowed Lewis' political rivals to undermine the overall scheme. When jail space was used as overflow housing for the springs' guests, Monroe County politicians like John Hutchinson influenced the move of the county court and jail facilities to the village of Union. The district court moved to Lewisburg. The public showed a reluctance to prevent the moves, and Fontville remained a dream.²

Accounts of the springs and the surrounding country are many and vivid in this early period. Among the most interesting accounts is the correspondence kept by then-Congressman (later U.S. Secretary of War) James McHenry. He wrote to his wife in September 1789 about the burial of a visitor and described the surrounding country:

> Mrs. Perry died on Sunday morning, and was intered yesterday afternoon. She was thought to be somewhat better on her arrival; but a few days shewed the fallacy of hopes founded on a strong expectation of the benefit from the waters...The burying ground is at a little from the springs, on the summit of a hill which is covered with large and shady oaks. I counted eleven graves, some inclosed with a kind of pailing, and the rest with large logs of timber, said to be intended as a security against wolves. I could not comtemplate the remains of the dead quietly resting in those rude impalements without a few mournful emotions... There is neither stone or monumental inscription to be seen to tell any thing respecting the dead.³

McHenry further described the Sweet Springs in 1789 as an "agreeable prospect" and consisting of a "mess house, a dwelling house, and a corn field."⁴ McHenry's record keeping was indicative of something that would happen many times throughout the 19th century: some guests died because some arrived sick.

Even McHenry was not in the best of health. He returned to the springs again in 1794, where he wrote his wife:

> I attended a Methodist sermon yesterday and heard card playing and dancing condemned as damnable sins. The sermon was scarcely ended when some of the gentlemen returned to the card-table, and others joined the ladies to receive their approbation for an assembly.[5]

McHenry was particularly partial to a church sermon. In a letter to his wife on August 24, 1794, McHenry remarked that he heard "a very animated sermon delivered by Bishop Maddison upon the excellency of the christian worship."[6] His statement and his remarks on gambling were strong testimony to McHenry's lobbying ability. Many visitors were gamesters, but most of the local populace abstained. It was doubtful that many of the local farmers could have mustered the needed funds to play with the springs' affluent guests.

No doubt preacher Francis Asbury's presence in the region a short time earlier had a pronounced effect on the local populace. In addition to the criticism of gaming, the springs region became a center of Methodist itinerant activity. Rehoboth Church, the first Methodist church west of the mountains, was built only a few miles south. The mixture of gaming and religion was noticeable to guests like McHenry.[7]

Even more eloquent was McHenry's description of the economic potential of Snake Run Valley, located a few miles northeast of Sweet Springs.

> Would you believe it that the medicinal waters of Snake-run and about two hundred and fifty acres of land containing all these interesting spectacles could be bought for about

L250. Whereas I have no doubt considering the probable progress of population and wealth that at no very remote period the purchase will require two or three thousand.[8]

For McHenry, it must have a lonely series of visits to the springs. In late September 1794, McHenry wrote that most of his fellow visitors had left. The springs become "a village deserted by its inhabitants whose houses are falling into ruin."[9]

McHenry's account of the poor conditions coincided with that of another visitor, Dabney Minor of Orange, Virginia. His 1799 letter to Virginia official John Brown, Jr., described living at the springs as "barely tolerable."[10] Minor came across as being as critical of the guests-an experience at great variance with McHenry's:

> There were about a dozen ladies among the number whose faces we never saw except at meal times. Stiff, formal and ceremonious in the extreme, the sight of them only served to raise sentiments of aversion and disgust. Nor were the men much better. In this society I dragged out three miserable days.[11]

McHenry and Minor's descriptions noted the condition of early life at the springs. However, changes became evident as time moved forward. Later travel accounts do not give the reader the feeling of a barren and wild terrain with no luxury.

In an 1804 journal of his vacation to Sweet Springs, Dinwiddie County resident John Howell Briggs described a cheerier setting. To him, the Sweet developed into a more fashionable vacation setting.

Briggs said the accommodations were superior to the White Sulphur Springs to the north.[12]

Gaming was more common and "gamesters," or professional billiards or card players, were a regular sight. Perhaps the most famous gamester of Sweet Springs was Robert Bailey, who in 1822 wrote a book on his own exploits at the tables. Bailey was not simply a gambler, as his journal maintains; he was rather a businessman with something to gain by popularizing the springs. He began to acquire much land around Barber's Creek as early as 1804, paying cash for his acquisitions. He knew taverns well; he had previously operated the Bell Tavern in Washington, D.C. Bailey's Tavern was built by 1821 along a stage road. Historian Robert Douthat Stoner called Bailey the "most noted tavernkeeper ever to own land in Botetourt."[13]

Other guests had more serious pursuits. Briggs was pleased to meet the Episcopal bishop James Madison during the clergyman's 1804 trip there. The cousin of the future President was an accomplished scientist as well as a religious figure.

> A man of great worth and talents..After his mornings ride,
> he frequently amused himself with some philosophical
> experiments; and as far as he could, he determined by chemical
> operations, the property of the waters here. I assisted him in
> some of them; and when the result of his experiments to writing,
> I made a transcript of them, which I still have.[14]

The waters of the springs had great healing properties, and Bishop Madison was only one of many to experiment with the spring water. Dr. John J. Moorman, resident physician at the White Sulphur

Springs, looked into its effects on various ailments. The Red Sweet Springs was good for neuralgia cases, according to Moorman. The iron salts made for a favorable bathing or drinking experience. It was not uncommon for a patient to undergo a series of springs, or a course, to alleviate his or her ailment. Tonics were prescribed. It is little wonder that Moorman wrote of the virtues of the springs as "an elasticity and buoyancy of body and spirit that makes one feel like leaping walls or clearing ditches at a single bound."[15]

Moorman's tracts wre published to promote tourism. He acknowledged his motivation, but he apparently wrote his tracts also to correct what he felt were inaccuracies in water treatment and healing properties:

> To correct these and many other abuses of this valuable
> water, I published various pamphlets designed to guide
> to valitidinarism in their safe and profitable use. Up to the
> time of the publication of these pamphlets, not a line have
> ever been published relative to their appropriate applicabilities
> or the proper methods of using them.[16]

The politician in Moorman continued the crusade:

> Seeing the good effects that resulted from these pioneer
> efforts, I published in 1846, a small ultimo entitled "Virginia
> Springs" treating not only of the White Sulphur, but also of all
> the mineral springs of the state.[17]

Madison was not the only religious figure to have seen the beauty of the springs. The Methodist itinerant preacher Lorenzo Dow was invited, and accosted, at the Sweet Springs. In 1813, he was invited to preach by an unnamed local churchman at the springs. Dow's fiery sermons in his preaching periodically offended people. When he preached at the Sweet, Dow was punched by a Charleston, South Carolina, man named Baker. The South Carolinian claimed that Dow had insulted his wife's honor in a sermon he had given nine years before.[18]

When William Lewis died in 1811, his son John took over operations of the springs. The younger Lewis possessed a strong personality and used it to full advantage. He won over many local farmers by freely lending money. The notations of loans in John Lewis' inventory revealed his generosity; notes and bonds due as far back as 1810 were still on the books at his death in 1823. Perhaps John Lewis expected he would collect them in time.[19]

In the 1820s Sweet Springs continued to entertain famous visitors, and better facilities were developed for their stays. The construction of a new and improved central hotel facility was a major priority. The creation of the main building was based on architectural design plans that reflected the style of Thomas Jefferson. According to historians, a Jeffersonian architect named William B. Phillips was likely to have worked on several porticos at both the springs and the University of Virginia. Planners hoped to complete a group of smaller buildings to surround the main hotel for extra occupancy, cooking, and stable facilities, but the completion of a handful of them took place almost a decade following Jefferson's death in 1826. Recent finds in the Monroe County Courthouse seem to verify that Jefferson had a major influence on the design of the main brick hotel.[20]

During the 1840s extensive work was completed on porticos and rooms at the Sweet Springs. John's son William Lynn Lewis realized that the competition for guests at the springs was fierce at times and added $60,000 both to improve the brick building's porticos and to add other tasteful features, such as black walnut staircases. The style was decidedly Greek. Chambers were expanded in size. Bad economic times interfered with some construction, however; the completion of the huge dining facility was delayed until 1850.[21]

Many of the guests who stayed at the hotel were quite famous, including the French supporter of the American Revolution Marquis de Lafayette, Thomas Jefferson, James Madison, Virginia politician Henry Clay, and Presidents Franklin Pierce and Millard Fillmore. Lafayette visited during his famous return tour of the United States in 1824. President Pierce arrived at the springs district in July 1854. Despite the colorful array of famous personalities, Frances Logan, in her book on the Sweet Springs stated that most visitors were well-to-do people from urban trading cities along the East Coast.[22]

There appeared to be a tour of spas whose final destination was the Sweet. The last week of August and first week of September was the fashionable time. The sojourn at the Sweet usually followed a tour of the White, Salt, or Red Sweet Springs for either their differing healing properties or as a way of "sampling" various forms of hospitality at the resorts.[23]

The concept of the healing spa vacation caught on, and other resorts were developed. Salt Sulphur Springs, fifteen to twenty miles southwest of the Sweet, was a popular resort hotel site by 1825. Ervin Benson had run guest cabins there, and his sons-in-law, Isaac Caruthers and William Erskine, transformed the enterprise into a resort, which drew a near monopoly of out-of-state visitors. Perhaps indicative of an underlying competitive hostility, South Carolinians preferred the Salt; Virginians always predominated at the Sweet.[24]

Another early spa was Red Sweet Springs, later called Sweet Chalybeate. Guests had stayed there as early as 1773, and Mark Pencil wrote in 1839 that the Red Sweet Springs was a run-down place. It was not helped economically by its close proximity to the popular Sweet Springs.[25]

Within a mile or two of the Sweet, wrote Pencil, they came to the Red Spring, "an old dilapidated building, grey with age, and all its windows shattered. A young country boy was swinging on the broken gate which led to the house from the road."[26] In an attempt to improve its prospects, the Red Sweet Company was formed in 1836.[27]

The Sweet Springs Company also incorporated the same year, and shares were sold at $100 apiece. In the 1840s and 1850s, new owners made the Red Sweet a sister resort to the Sweet Springs. A man named Bias promoted the Red Sweet Springs in concert with the nearby Sweet. The Red Sweet Springs offered pools for both men and women, and Bias stocked a day room with newspapers from varying regions, which no other springs could claim. These subtle differences resulted in good business for Bias.[28]

The Royall Case

The springs served as a gathering place for settling disputes of many kinds. In a variety of court cases, area witnesses gathered at the familiar Sweet. One of the controversial of the area's cases was that of the disputed will of Major William Royall. In the course of events, there were hints that his wife may have hastened the major's death. It was an ugly situation that put many local loyalties to the test.

When the Major died in December 1812, his wife Anne presented a will that clearly intended his estate for her. The major's niece, Elizabeth Roane and her husband James, quickly challenged the will. Roane felt that the will was phony and had been witnessed after the major's death. The two witnesses to the will were farmer James Wiley and Anne Royall's mother, Mary Butler. Roane's grounds for the suit centered around the attestation of witnesses to the paper. The Roanes believed there were mistakes on the instrument itself. The original case was heard in the summer of 1814; subsequently papers were filed for an appeal at the District Chancery Court in Staunton.[29]

William Herbert and Michael Aritt, justices of the peace appointed to take testimony from the area's citizens, came to the house of John Lewis to gather their depositions. On July 15, the Shawvers, owners of a tavern, were the first to be interviewed. Elizabeth Shawver had visited the Royall house often, but only as long as the major was alive. She claimed she saw the household servants "by the direction of his wife tye him & take him to the house by force."[30]

Jacob Shawver shaved the major regularly at Royall's home. Anne had told Shawver she was afraid of John Lewis. After the major's death, she told Shawver to notify James Wiley to prepare himself for court to validate the witnessing of the will. Wiley was angered when Shawver told him of this fact, and further stated to the deponent that he knew nothing about the will. To cloud the situation further, the spelling of the farmer's last name was different on the document than from his normal signature. Local farmer James Nesbit Linton claimed he saw a servant girl who had been sent by Anne verbally abuse the major. Linton came to the major's defense and threatened to whip the servant. This sent the girl back to the house, but Anne ordered Linton off the property. Linton further stated that the major had told him that he had intended his estate to go to his nephew, William Roane.[31]

It is evident that Anne Royall was much at odds with her neighbors. She eventually lost the case, which had gone on for two years. It had started at Fincastle in April 1817, and she became disillusioned and sold off most of the land to James Wiley long before the suit was settled in 1819. Wiley became party to the suit with Anne as he had interest in the Royall estate. However, judgement invalidated William Royall's will. In addition both William Royall and James Wiley had borrowed from the rising mercantilist Andrew Beirne of Union. Wiley had to file against Anne to cover his bill to Beirne.[32]

The Royall Case brought out more than angry litigants. A peculiar regional status network was at work. Society connections, friendships, and kinship mattered in the mounting neighborhood sentiment against Anne Royall. One of the major's most valuable properties was a 480-acre tract of land that adjoined the land of John Lewis near the Sweet Springs. Lewis indeed disliked Anne for stated premarital relations with the major. He had no wish to be her neighbor in the center of Lewis land holdings. The irony lay in the fact that Anne had once been a friend of the Lewis family. Anne's mother Mary had been a servant at the Lewis home, the Wigwam. Lewis, perhaps seeing Anne as a member of a different social class, gradually came to resent her influence over the major. In any case he believed she was capable of forging the will. To further injure her character, Lewis claimed that Anne was Royall's "concubine, after which it was said he married her twice."[33]

Another unseen point in the Royall Case was John Lewis' influence through patronage. A community benefactor (Lewis) who kindly lent money was more likely to garner positive public opinion than an aristocratic hermit (Royall) and his Pennsylvania-born wife. The Sweet Springs was a logical, but not neutral, place to gather depositions. Anne's abraisive personality hurt her character references in the case. She was strong willed and known for her quick temper. Despite Anne's fading fortunes, James Wiley's constant support appeared loyal. His support notwithstanding, it is improbable that the flurry of accounts against her could have represented a conspiracy. While the Lintons and Shawvers lived in close proximity, the depositions of George and Elizabeth Carson were taken in the more neutral environment of Cumberland County, Virginia, in March 1815.[34]

It would be short-sighted to characterize this court case simply as a group of farmers closing ranks on the widow. Among most local farmers generally, Anne was supported and not chastised. She enjoyed success and suffered failure at many stages of her long career in journalism. But it was not a surprise to western Virginians some years later when Anne was accused of being a "common scold."[35]

The presence of the Royalls did have some positive impact on the local populace. One success story that emerged from an association with the Royalls was the career of Matthew Dunbar. Matthew's father had bought a large farming tract near the village of Rocky Point (now Sinks Grove) in Monroe County in 1793. It was likely this family is a branch of Dunbars of Gap Mills. Matthew, the eldest son, was enrolled in Dr. McElhenney's school around 1810. The Presbyterian minister taught him the roots of law, which whetted Dunbar's taste for debate. Dunbar studied many long hours in Major Royall's library. His friendship with Anne continued long after the major's death. Her letters to him were prominently featured in her later travel journal, *Travels in Alabama*. In 1815 Dunbar left Gap Mills to study in Kanawha County. He was admitted to the bar three years later and became the prosecuting attorney and later served as a circuit judge. He died in 1859 owing his literary advances to the Royalls and his schooling in the Presbyterian Church.[36]

After John Lewis

Others in this area prospered as well. When John Lewis died in 1823, his will was six pages long. It included a codicil by which he bequeathed additional land to the heir of Sweet Springs, William Lynn Lewis. An accompanying list of bonds and notes indicated that Potts Creek Valley farmers and tradesmen, including Field Jarvis, Jacob Shawver, and James Smith, had been indebted to him prior to 1810. Covington innkeeper Dennis Callaghan was indebted to John Lewis by a supply order. From this document it is evident why John Lewis was the local power.[37]

The Lewis family were the patriarchs of the community for other reasons as well. The nation's upper class were drawn to the Springs in part by the owners themselves. The Lewises married well. John had married Jane Thomson of South Carolina, and after her death, had wed Mary Preston of the prominent Virginia family. One of John's daughters, Mary Sophia, married James Woodville, who was related to Virginia politician Andrew Stevenson. William Lynn Lewis married twice. His second wife was Lettie Floyd, daughter of a Virginia governor John Floyd. On August 16, 1837, Governor Floyd died while visiting his daughter at the springs. He was buried in the Lewis family cemetery at the springs. A large manse called Lynnside was built to replace the primitive Wigwam. The family connections helped, but the springs were known primarily for their healthy waters, and they brought many visitors.[38]

William Lynn Lewis was deeply involved in the burgeoning cotton trade in the lower South. When the slave trade increased in 1820s Alabama and Louisiana, Lewis acquired land in those states. He lived in South Carolina for several years, but returned to live at Lynnside in 1848. Four years later the Sweet Springs were sold to a company headed by Oliver Beirne, Allen Taylor Caperton, and John Echols. All three men were residents of the town of Union, Virginia.[39]

Allen Taylor Caperton became active in other springs enterprises. In 1853, he became one of four owners of the White Sulphur Springs. The former owner, James Calwell, had died two years earlier, which assured Caperton dominance of the "circuit" of two large springs. The sale of the Sweet Springs in 1852 marked the end of the Lewis-Union power feud. The feud started in 1807, when William Lewis lost his courthouse political base. The Lewis family influence faded to other business personalities.[40]

The Capertons, Beirnes, and Lewises were serious businessmen. In many local estate settlements, they were owed or assigned something in the final tally. Andrew Beirne's meteoric rise from a door-to-door ginseng salesman to a top local merchant and landowner. When James N. Linton of Potts Creek died in 1849, he left behind a large number of debt slips to various individuals. One particularly large indebtedness was a $49.17 certificate owed to the estate of Allen's father Hugh Caperton, who had died shortly before Linton.[41]

Business aside, Sweet Springs was also a place to resolve estate differences. Other estate settlements were simply botched by executors. When James Linton's brother John died in 1839, executor and tavern keep William Booth, Sr., sued his own son and the heirs of Linton! The Lintons and William Booth, Jr. felt the tavernkeeper had misused his role as executor. On June 15, 1843, witnesses gathered at the Brick Hotel of the Sweet Springs to give their testimony. The witnesses in this case were John Jarvis, William Humphries, Joseph Deeds, Francis A. Wiley, John S. Wiley, James Carson, John Wolf, Andrew Wilson, Alexander Rayhill, John Anders, and Elizabeth Linton. The case remained unresolved for several years.[42]

The most common type of court case heard at the Sweet Springs Courthouse was that of a sour land deal. For instance, Field A. Jarvis sued John Dodd over a piece of property on Potts Creek sold to the latter in 1843. The price of the land was $600, to be paid in six annual installments each Christmas of $100 each. Dodd did not abide by the terms of the agreement. Instead, Dodd sent an installment payment of $15 in 1844. He furthermore failed to send in timely installments. The situation was further complicated when the land was sold at public auction. A decree was posted on the doors of both the Monroe County Court House and Sweet Springs prior to the land sale, on August 29, 1847. The land was purchased by Joseph A. Alderson, with John Hutchinson booking the security money for the purchase.[43]

The issue was finally settled in the Monroe County Circuit Superior Court of Chancery in 1849. Dodd was forced to pay the full cost of the land with interest. The commissioner of the public auction, George W. Hutchinson, was credited his commission for the sale. John Hutchinson was the Monroe County Clerk as well as security to Alderson. The latter two received their bonds back.[44]

It is curious that Alderson and the two Hutchinsons were interested in the land on Potts Creek at all. For years, this was Lewis territory, and the Hutchinson family was interested primarily in the promotion of the county seat at Union. This case indirectly indicated that the Lewis political influence was on the wane.[45]

The 1852 sale of the Sweet Springs Company was an ending and a beginning. Beirne, Caperton, and Echols proved to be excellent promoters. They enhanced various travel tracts such as the 1851 *A Guide to the Virginia Springs* by Dr. J.J. Moorman, the resident physician at White Sulphur Springs of Greenbrier County. Although most of the book was a study of all the area springs and their mineral composition, ample space was devoted to various descriptions of travel routes to get there. Moorman's booklet also described the springs to potential vacationers.[46]

Of Sweet Springs, Moorman wrote:

The water of the spring rises into a large cylindrical reservoir,
from opposite sides of which it flows out by small pipes;
one conveying water to the bath for the men, the other to that
for the ladies. The men's bath is of a quadrangular
form, surrounded by a wall, and open at the top. It is of
tolerable extent and clear-the bottom being of gravel, and
the water constantly passing out, after it reaches a certain height.[47]

To further entice vacationers, architects were brought in to lay out brick villas. Even though the villas were not completed, more colorful promotional materials included them. The German artist Edward Beyer portrayed the villas as well as three hotels (the main one known as the Brick or Jefferson Hotel) in his impressive landscape painting of the Sweet Springs in 1857. This was likely what the Sweet Springs Company wanted but never achieved. Beyer's *Album of Virginia* of that year included many promotional landscapes of area springs.[48]

The success of that promotion was reflected in the Sweet Springs account book. In 1857 the ledgers reflected that much money was paid out by the springs to other hands. The outgoing drafts and checks that year amounted to over twenty thousand dollars. Much was spent on repairs, gaming devices, and blankets. They even spent good money on spittoons for the gaming rooms.[49]

The lure of the springs was still popular when the Civil War broke out, but the local political power enjoyed during the years of Lewis ownership was not the same. The three men who ran the Sweet Springs Company had extended their domain from the town of Union to the country beyond. The close bonds John Lewis had made with the local farmers were not maintained.

Chapter 3. Bottles and Politics: Temperance and Political Movements

In 1856, William Booth sold his tavern on the old Fincastle-Sweet Springs Turnpike to David Givens.[1] Located on a well-traveled turnpike to nearby spring, it had been a successful dining establishment for many years. Because of "Mr. Booth's desire for liquor," however, "the business ran down."[2] Although the property changed hands, the sale did not end Booth's downfall. The new proprietor was not averse to Booth visiting, and *drinking*, in his tavern. The rest of the story is predictable:

> ..plenty of old corn whiskey, apple and peach brandy. He [Givens] played a high and at cards, and William Booth, having an appetite for strong drink, also played a good game of cards and was a frequent visitor at the Given's Tavern. Night after night they played. Large sums of money were put up and while Booth was a good player, he was no match for Givens, he won and won, until it was said, he had won back the full amount he had paid Booth for the property, and eventually the Boothes became very poor.[3]

William Booth had once been an able businessman; he and his family had run the tavern on Potts Creek successfully for more than thirty years. However, his predicament was common. The region's winter nights were often cold and drafty. The weary farmer and the visiting traveler often found solace in a warming glass of corn whiskey or brandy. Organized resistance to alcoholic drink was to face an uphill

Political Steel Engraving (c. 1853) showing President Franklin Pierce surrounded by past Presidents. Author's Collections.

battle in the region.

Excessive drinking on the part of its residents and visitors caused considerable public embarrassment for entire counties. But In December 1827, concerned citizens of Alleghany County circulated a petition on a drinker matter and sent it to the Virginia House of Delegates on a drinking matter in Alleghany County. Local citizen Jacob Persinger and a man named John Gill apparently had stabbed a gentlemen named Pattison. The petition signers pleaded that Persinger should be spared a two-year prison sentence due to his advanced age and large, poverty-stricken family. The Alleghany citizens further stated: "the said Persinger, Gill & Pattison were all intoxicated, that the chief testimony against the accused was the indistinct recollections of Pattison."[4] The memorial stated that the offense was reported to have been committed by Gill, who was not sentenced. It also declared Persinger innocent. The petition was signed by some leading citizens of Covington and the a long, narrow valley known as the Rich Patch, south of the town and Persinger's neighborhood. The signatures included George Mallow, John Tyree, James Merry, Jesse Humphries, and Henry Bailey Greenwood. The Potts Creek Valley farmers signed nearly to a man. Affidavits were written by Mallow and Hugh Paul Taylor to assure the Delegates of Persinger's good character.[5]

This strong showing was mounted not simply to rescue a friend, but to more importantly, to insulate a young Alleghany County against political reprisals over a drunken fight. The fact that a memorial was sent to the Virginia Legislature signified the importance of the case. Pattison was an outsider and the memorialists stood by their own fellow countians. The county was only five years old and had to slow its ability to resolve its own jurisdictional troubles, where they involved alcohol or not.⁶

The Sons of Temperance of North America discovered Alleghany County in the late 1840s. Some twenty years before, the idea had been formulated of a temperance league to assist the working man in the production of his labors. The Sons were one of the most organized leagues. Most of their work in the 1830s centered in New England and New York. As in those places in its early period, temperance went hand in hand with religion in western Virginia; however, good productivity was the focus of the Sons of Temperance. A sober man could better provide for his family and society, the theory was, if he avoided drink. The first wave of this evangelical movement died down with little effect in the mountainous counties.⁷

The evangelical and political temperance movements were more successful in other areas. Some thirty miles east of Covington, Lexington candidates frequently used liquor to bribe grateful citizens for their votes. Town reformers denounced this practice and formed "cold water armies."⁸

Lewisburg had a strong Presbyterian influence. In 1829, John McElhenney and other town fathers formed a Bible Society that produced many temperance tracts by the 1840s. In the same year, its own temperance group was formed. The Baptist and Presbyterian clergy of Monroe and Greenbrier Counties were influential enough to endorse temperance regularly in the 1830s.⁹

The Indian Creek Church south of Union in Monroe had a large temperance-minded following. A formal temperance society stretched as far as Union, where, in 1849, the town built a frame structure to serve as a temperance hall on Main Street. The construction of the hall reflected the county's concern for temperance.¹⁰

Its organization efforts brought success to the temperance movement in general. The Virginia Society for the Promotion of Temperance brought reformers and churchmen together in 1826. Locally, the Sons of Temperance's Grand Division of Virginia formed a new division, Number 244 in Covington. Its surviving journal, which ran from 1849 to 1852, proved how hard it was to induce and convince mountain men to stay on the wagon. In 1849, 36 men took the pledge to abstain from the use of spirits. Of those men, six violated the pledge and four withdrew their pledges.[11]

The social composition of the pledges included businessmen and local officials. These men-owners and proprietors-led by example. Thompson McAllister, a pillar of the Alleghany business community, took the pledge on February 15, 1850. William Scott, a tavern and innkeeper himself, pledged in 1849. James Rogers who had invested in the turnpike boom, was a pledge in 1849. Andrew Damron was Alleghany County surveyor from 1833 to 1850, a county justice in 1838, and local delegate from 1850 to 1851. John L. Pitzer was a justice in 1846. The list of society officers in 1849 included Andrew Damron, Samuel F. Few, S.J. Baker, John L. Pitzer, John Robinson, William Scott, Hiram Baker, Leo Rosenham, George Matheny, John Carter, William Bishop, C.E. Farmer, Thomas Stillings, William Printz, Silas Vines, and James Rodgers.[12]

Perhaps more important than society membership was the money lost to the county through the lack of taxes and licensing fees. By the late 1850s, tougher licensing laws had only partially succeeded to some extent. A petition of 185 Alleghany County signatures was sent to the Virginia Legislature in February 1853 by citizens who felt the licensing process laws were defective at the county level and that licenses could be better issued from the county or corporation courts. The Sons of Temperance were the first signers, but several middle-class Rich Patch farmers signed, too. The licensing petition was not popular in the Potts Creek Valley but very much so in Covington. The county leaders had effected a political shift towards temperance.[13]

The social composition of Number 244 included some of the local mountain yeomen farmers. However, it was difficult to join the group. A Committee of Vigilance surveyed and voted on the applicant's character. Henry B. Rose, a student of about 20 years of age when he applied to be a member of the Sons of Temperance in the summer of 1850, was scrutinized and voted in. A few of the local members came from Potts Creek and the Rich Patch, but most were from the town of Covington.[14] The strict membership rules were enforced to maintain general appearances to the public at large. The Sons of Temperance of North America was a centralized organization to be looked upon with respect and honor. If that honor were smudged, the national leaders could hardly take Covington seriously in its fight against the bottle. Members were never numerous, and it was far easier to be removed then to be admitted. An officer could ask for an investigation of a member (or brother, as they called themselves) for the non-payment of dues or suspected drinking. According to the group's journal, Hiram Baker asked for an investigation of Charles Fridley for not paying his dues in 1850.[15]

The Sons were secretive, but they had a public image to maintain in patriotic ways as well. On July 1, 1850, they were busy planning a parade and ceremony at a town church for the 4th of July. This was a great source of exposure and excitement for the members. For months prior to the event, they had been preparing a special banner and Bible to present at the ceremony. It was a special honor to speak at the event, which was to include the reciting of the Declaration of Independence. On this occasion, Samuel Few received the honor of the recitation, and Thompson McAllister read from various patriotic tracts. Except for these special public occasions, however, the Sons of Temperance local kept secret their meetings within the walls of the Alleghany County Court House.[16]

Members of local organizations also attended national or state association meetings to show their support for the cause. The state organization of the Sons of Temperance held its 1852 summer meeting in Fincastle. Andrew Damron and John L. Pitzer represented Chapter 244 at the function. Attendance at the regional function was an important factor in statewide recognition; if the local did not send representatives, the area's campaign was considered lacking to the overall organization. Other temperance organizations in the region did not have the social connections or tight unity that the Sons had, and they foundered.[17]

The contributions of the Sons of Temperance in the region helped shield some Alleghany County and area residents from the same horrible fate suffered by William Booth. By the time of the Civil War, the Sons could claim something of a victory. At a general temperance meeting in 1854, a report included both Craig and Alleghany Counties as jurisdictions that had stopped issuing licenses to taverns for retail liquor. The report noted the same status of 34 other Virginia counties.[18]

<u>Politics</u>

The issues of drinking became a small part of a growing political awareness in the region. The Sons of Temperance stated an approach to the phenomenon, reaching larger political venues by use of a united political cause. The pageantry and patriotism enjoyed by the organization were similar to the festivities of the political contests held in the region during the 1840s and 1850s. Politics was a privilege, and so was the vote. Yeomen farmers would travel for miles, sometimes quite a few miles, simply to cast a vote for the candidate of their choice. This was not surprising; for many years, the western Virginian had been a political non-entity due to the whims of the eastern planters.

The struggle of western Virginia was a long one. The weight of the easterners, power was felt in the Virginia Constitutional Convention of 1829-30, from which the angry westerners came away with little but contempt. Despite the growth of western Virginia, the easterners wanted no change that would sway power away from their overall control. They opposed the western representatives call for internal improvements and wide suffrage.[19]

Political parties became the focal point of western Virginia hopes for overall prosperity. The polls and the election campaigns were social events complete with parades and fireworks for those who could vote. The Whigs were more economically inclined. Their credo was the "American System" of Henry Clay, a grand design of interregional economic unity through improvements and protective tariff rates for imports. The Democrats were against such high tariffs and expensive improvements at the national level.[20]

In western Virginia-as in many parts of the new country-local governments did not always support a popular national figure like Henry Clay or Andrew Jackson. Greenbrier County was solidly Whig in the 1830s. Monroe County elected several prominent Clayite Whigs.

These men looked to mountain and western Whigs in the national sphere, such as Tennessee's Hugh Lawson White and Henry Clay. Alleghany County voted predominantly Democrat, but had a political history peppered with a strong, local Whig presence. The focus on transportation was popular in the mountains. In truth, class structure still appeared to determine much of the political aims of the region. Many of those who voted Whig were well-to-do people. Many farmers were loyal to Democrat Andrew Jackson; they identified with the orphaned youth who improved his station by hard work. However, trade centers like Lewisburg adhered to much of the Whig doctrine.[21]

Western Virginia's troubles with the east developed into a regional Whiggish outlook in some areas. Certain areas did not feel the dominent Democratic Legislature favored them. For instance in 1832-33, states rights became an issue when South Carolina declared a high tariff unconstitutional. In Greenbrier County, the population voted heavily against South Carolinian politician John C. Calhoun's attempts to call the federal tariff "null and void" within a state jurisdiction. Lewisburg residents held a dinner to honor the pro-union Virginian William Cabell Rives in 1833 and denounce Calhoun's position. Rives came to embody the Whig's union outlook. John Goode, a resident of Craig's Creek in Botetourt (later Craig) County and a self-proclaimed Henry Clay-style Whig, stated, "I was always opposed to states rights and nullification."[22] The Greenbrier Whigs were strongly supported because of their stance on transportation improvements. As Lewisburg was one of the next towns to benefit from the building of the James River and Kanawha Canal, politics became a natural stage on which to lobby the issue. Despite its political activity, however, Lewisburg never got the canal; they had issue solidarity, if not improvements.

Leaders such as Ballard Smith were firmly allied to Whigs of national stature, such as William Ballard Preston of Blacksburg. Henry Erskine was a presidential elector for Hugh Lawson White of Tennessee in 1836, when the ticket was known as the "Republican Whig Ticket."[23]

Local politicians of Whig extraction were not hard to find. Hugh Caperton and his son Allen Taylor Caperton were two of the best-known Whigs. Hugh, born in Greenbrier County on April 17, 1781, served as sheriff of Monroe County in 1805 and as a delegate from 1810 to 1813 and 1826 to 1830. He served in the U.S. House of Representatives from 1813 to 1815, where he met Henry Clay. Springs entrepreneur and politician Allen Taylor Caperton was born November 21, 1810, and was educated at both the University of Virginia and Yale. He graduated from the latter institution in 1832. He served in the Virginia House of Delegates from 1841 to 1842 and 1857 to 1861, and in the U.S. Congress shortly before his death in 1876.[24]

Henry Clay's ties to the region revolved around a number of friendships. He stayed primarily at White Sulphur Springs due to his connections with owner James Calwell, a gentleman originally from Baltimore. Calwell arrived in 1817 to take proprietorship of the White Sulphur and became fast friends with the statesman. Clay found himself engulfed by Calwell's hospitality many times, but, unlike many famous guests, he stayed only for brief visits and not for an entire "circuit." In 1832, he came to the springs with a large retinue consisting of his wife, their grandson, four servants, and a large dog.[25]

Even in the calm atmosphere of the springs, Clay's political life placed demands on his attention. His political enemies also occasionally stayed at the springs. Of a chance encounter with Andrew Stevenson at White Sulphur, physician John Moorman wrote in his journal:

> [Clay] seemed to take delight in meeting and outfacing them ..Mr. Clay deferred an intended call upon Colonel and Mrs. Singleton until he knew that Mr. Stevenson and other of his enemies were in Colonel's room, when he boldly walked in among them. Passing through the group without the slightest recognition of them..keeping up a lively conversation until all his enemies withdrew..[26]

Ample evidence in Clay's letters to Calwell show that he looked forward to his visits and local entertainments. He once wrote to Calwell:

> I shall leave [Staunton] today and I expect to arrive at the Warm Springs on Tuesday night, on Wednesday night at Callahans, and on Thursday evening at the White Sulphur Springs. Will you have the goodness to drop me a line to meet me at Callahans' informing me of the prospect of accommodations?[27]

Clay was a frequent visitor on the "springs tour," and often the guest of local Whigs. He had close ties to the Caperton family, and Allen Taylor Caperton was known as a particularly loyal ally of Clay. His father, Hugh, who had opened his home in Union, "Elmwood," to "Harry of the West" for a visit around 1845, was an official of the James River & Kanawha Company and had formerly served with Clay in the U.S.Congress. The room Clay stayed in has since been called

"Mr. Clay's Room." Clay left behind some souvenirs to acknowledge the Caperton's hospitality. He gave his host a lock of his hair and a pinch of snuff from a box supposedly owned at one time by Czar Peter the Great of Russia.[28]

The Bank of the United States was a strong political issue in western Virginia. President Jackson was chronically opposed to the renewal of the charter of the Bank. Clay allied with local politicians were especially interested in this debate. Lewisburg resident Dr. Charles L. Peyton, a great-nephew of Thomas Jefferson, was one of Clay's strong allies on this issue. In May 1841, Clay wrote Peyton urging patience on reinstituting the defunct Bank of the United State. Clay did not count Virginia as a state stronghold for the charter's renewal. The Whiggish Peyton was very agitated over his state's hesitation.[29]

The Democratic Party, which favored the banking and political policies of President Andrew Jackson, had its advocates in the region. They released a number of broadsides and pamphlets warning against the dangers in the philosophy of the Whig Party. An 1840 broadside from the Botetourt Central Democratic Committee warned about the "British" Whig Party, which seemed to hark back to similar remarks regarding the extinct Federalist Party. Most of the members of the committee-namely Benjamin Carper, Thomas N. Burwell, John W. Thompson, Oliver Callaghan, George W. Wilson, Jacob Woltz, James Paxton, and James McDowell-were residents of Fincastle. Despite their location in the valley, they reached out to the mountain farmer with a tone of urgency: "Come out then from your Hills and your Dales, your Vallies and Mountains..RALLY as you did in the days of yore under the REPUBLICAN FLAG.."[30]

Voting privilege was major issue in antebellum western Virginia. In 1835, a white male of 21 years or older could vote (1) if he owned 25 acres of land with a house, (2) a minimum of 50 acres of unimproved land, or (3) a house in a town lot, each with a minimum of six months ownership. This precluded from voting many farmers who did not have property or money. It favored the wealthier town dwellers and prevented many new arrivals from voting. This was a sectional problem that would not be resolved until 1851. By that time, the issue of a politically-divided Virginia was largely overshadowed by regional secession.[31]

There was surprising participation in political parties in the 1840s and 1850s. A broadside of the 1840 Whig Convention in Richmond listed 17 Alleghany and 19 Monroe County delegates who participated in the procession that gathered at Columbian Tavern. A number of existing records indicate in part how the region voted, but one complete set of papers exists in Monroe County for the governor's election of December 1851. The Whig candidate, George W. Summers, received 703 votes, and his Democratic opponent, Joseph Johnson, received 520. Both men were western Virginians. In the end, Johnson won the election statewide. An analysis of the Monroe vote reveals some interesting details of the polling places.[32]

The vote was usually held at a house or tavern and the county courthouse. On December 8, 1851, voters in one area of the county cast their ballots either at the tavern of David G. Givens or the house of Jacob Wickline, depending on whether the voter was a Democrat (Wickline's) or a Whig (Givens's). Givens also hosted the balloting for attorney general candidates of both parties for his region. Committees were appointed to oversee the vote and to ensure the accuracy of the count.³³

There were other interesting features of the vote. There was at least a sign of "family block" voting. The community leaders of the lower Potts Creek region-near the present-day community of Paint Bank-greatly favored the Whig candidates for governor. The following known residents of the community voted for Summers: William Arthur, James Carpenter, Charles Counts, Field A. Jarvis, Field W. Jarvis, John Jarvis, William Fletcher Jarvis, William Rowan, and Samuel Rusk.³⁴

Whether family members voted alike by agreement or by coincidence of interests is unknown, but there was a great deal of family voting in the 1851 gubernatorial election. Field W. Jarvis and Willliam Fletcher Jarvis were John's sons. Rusk was also a distant cousin. Rowan and Arthur were community leaders. All of these men were well to do, and most had large amounts of money or land. The Jarvis family owned much land near the Sweet Springs and Price's Mountain Turnpike. Rowan lived right along the Sweet Springs stage road, and Counts, Carpenter, and Arthur also lived very close to it. Between them there was much capital in the economic survival of the transport improvements along their road.³⁵

Another obvious Whig pocket was found in the Gap Mills-Sweet Springs area on the other side of Peter's Mountain. Included in this group were: George Bruffy, Calvin Campbell, Clemons K. Campbell, William G. Cook, John Dunbar, Robert Dunbar, Robert H. Dunbar, William Dunbar, Thomas W. Neel, William Neel, William Patton, James Parker, George Steele, and Daniel Worsham.³⁶ These were also well-to-do people. Mostly Presbyterian in stock, they were united by both blood and investment. The Dunbars were cousins of the Jarvis family. William Dunbar married the sister of Field A. and John Jarvis. William Neel married another Jarvis sister. James Parker's grandson James Bostic married into the Jarvis family. The Steeles, Pattons, and Campbells were interrelated. The Steeles also married into the Dunbar family. George Bruffy was a minister who was also related to the families. The sole exceptions to this particular family bloc vote in this community were William G. Cook and Daniel Worsham. Cook was an educated doctor who went to medical school in Baltimore and settled at the Sweet Springs in 1851. Worsham was also a resident there. Their interests were geared more towards Whiggish tendencies rather than a family vote.[37]

While perhaps not intentionally the same vote, the Jarvis-Dunbar bloc vote of 1851 netted George W. Summers a total of 16 votes. There were exceptions. William R. Neel and Daniel Neel voted for Johnson, as did Campbell Steele. However, this "defection" was a minority in their bloc. The same Jarvis-Dunbar bloc voted similarly for Sidney S. Baxter in the attorney general's race that same day. Countywide, Baxter and his opponent tied with 504 votes apiece.[38]

The Jarvis-Dunbar bloc vote secured for Summers only the region between Gap Mills and Potts Mountain. Some miles south, in the Monroe County seat of Union, the Beirnes and Alexanders proudly voted

Table 2. The Jarvis-Dunbar Block Vote of 1851 by Relation of Direct Line from Field Jarvis.[39]
Please note this is not a comprehensive genealogical table, only a partial bloodline with voters in the 1851 election.

Field Jarvis m. Asenith Adams
(1756-1839)
Their children:
John* m. Margaret Dunbar
(1791-1870)
sons William Fletcher*
    Field W.*
Field A.*
(1800-1890) m. Sally Ervine
Susannah m. John Barton Linton
 son George A.*
Nancy m. William Dunbar*
sons Robert*
    John A.*@

Mary Ann m. William H. Neel*

*voted for G.W. Summers
*@ Possibly voted for Summers

for Johnson. In fairness, the vote of all community leaders did not automatically shift to Summers. With the candidate himself was his party. The Whigs were breaking apart by 1851, as President Taylor had died in the preceding year. Summers and John Minor Botts represented a nationalistic wing of the party. The Democrats still held a firm grip on states rights, which appealed to part of the local elite.[40]

    The families who comprised the local elite also made a Whig dynasty of sorts. Hugh Caperton and his son Allen Taylor Caperton were prominent Whigs in Monroe County. Hugh's wife was Jane Erskine, was part of another prominent Whig family from Salt Sulphur Springs. James Francis Preston, brother of William Ballard Preston, married Hugh Caperton's daughter Sarah. William Preston went on to national politics, but James Preston represented Montgomery County in the state house.[41]

A recent study by Kenneth W. Noe indicates that Monroe County and neighboring Greenbrier County voted Whig for a long period of time. Noe found that key county political figures and grass-roots elite often determined the county vote. The elite was comprised of wealthy farmers and industry men. Allen Taylor Caperton was one of Monroe County's key political figures. Then again, if the county elite assisted the common farmer Whig vote in some fashion, it was not certain.[42]

Sectionalism played a large part in Virginia party politics. The eastern Democrats, headed by editor Thomas Ritchie, differed with many westerners in their party over issues of the National Bank, transportation improvements, the annexation of Texas, and slavery. The 1844 presidential election brought out the ugliness of this debate. Ritchie wrote of his fears that the "slaves of Angus McDonald," or white subsistence farmers, would win Virginia for Clay. These fears were unfounded. However, the rivalry within the Northern and Southern parts of the Democratic Party between former President Martin Van Buren and South Carolinian John C. Calhoun brought out some regional tension. Apparently "Little Tennessee," as the Virginia backcountry was sometimes called, was not inclined to support Martin Van Buren. Party newspapers went to work. The *Abingdon Banner* brought up Calhoun's nullification premise and stated "coals would be carried" to New Castle to convince Democratic voters to support Van

Buren. In 1844 Tennessean James Knox Polk was the resulting Democratic candidate, and the Whigs nominated Henry Clay.[43]

Noe's study looked at the situation in the 1855 gubernatorial election. The Whigs had died out as a political party. In its place, several new political parties emerged. The Republican Party attracted many of the northern and midwest Whigs. Another alternative organization was the single-issue the American Party, better known as the "Know Nothing" Party after its secret password. Anti-Catholic in nature, this political movement thrived in cities through the efforts of various patriotic and Protestant groups. The American Party was already an existing party, but gained essential membership only after the Whigs collapsed.[44]

In Virginia, American Party influence spread over the mountain counties, but only pockets of real support developed. Monroe and Greenbrier Counties voted for the American Party candidate for governor, Thomas S. Flournoy, in May 1855. Unfortunately for Flournoy, Democrat Henry A. Wise was his opponent. Wise received a great deal of support from the other mountain counties. The American Party was rendered powerless locally following this vote. Even the presence of Tennessean Andrew Jackson Donelson, the former President's adopted nephew, could not salvage the American Party in the presidential election of 1856. The local citizens of the Potts Valley and environs turned to more conventional, multi-issue parties.[45]

Citizen Petitions

Although they took their politics seriously, the local mountain

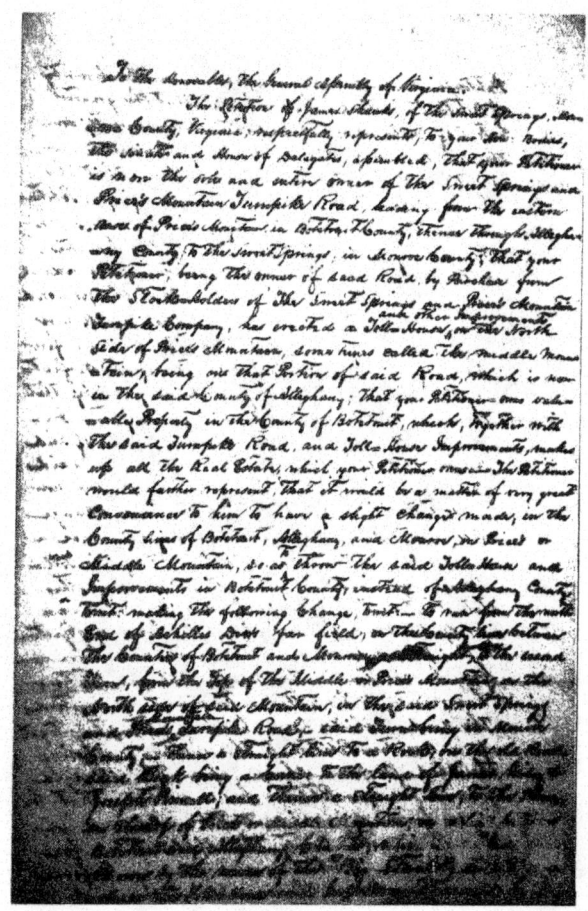

Legislative Petition: This one was against the formation of Craig County. Many opposed the new county due to the distance or costs of supporting public buildings. Courtesy: VA State Library. Photograph by Glenn Vogel.

citizenry felt far from Washington and Richmond. However, they did not hesitate to send official petitions, or memorials, to Richmond for the advantageous resolution of a local political quandary. One such issue was the formation of Craig County, Virginia. By 1846 it was apparent to the local citizenry that a new county was to be formed from various parts of Monroe, Alleghany, Giles, and Botetourt Counties. The Potts Valley farmers, particularly those in the southern portion near Sweet Springs, fell within the proposed borders of the new county. In December 1846, December 1849, and January 1850 the farmers petitioned the Virginia General Assembly on the matter. The new courthouse and public buildings needed in the new county seat would drive up costs and would not be any closer to them. In fact, the memorialists stated that the journey to the new public buildings would require a seven-mile journey over Potts Mountain. The 1850 petition was signed by 32 of these farmers, who claimed that it would be "unjust to be forced to leave our beloved county."[46]

Members of the General Assembly knew full well what the petitioners meant by this statement. In 1850, the county was the unit that held together the political and social fabric of western Virginia. Monroe Countians had connected with the same familiar politicians and institutions for many years in Union and Sweet Springs. Alleghany County farmers had contacts in Covington who knew their special interests. The elite in each county valued a small farmer on reciprocation. Perhaps he would vote a certain way on a local issue. A small farmer would spend many years establishing contacts for the loans, goods, and services that he needed. The cost of new public buildings was a real problem, but the greater concern was the loss of the security in their local elite.

Border setting was also a thorny issue. In the case of these farmers, it did not work in their favor. Although a vote was taken in December 1850 to consider public opinion, Craig County took many of the petitioners in its borders two years later. In December 1841, James Wiley and Margaret Shawver petitioned to stay within the borders of Alleghany County. In their communication they included a detailed map, which suggested that the county line be drawn at a sugar tree behind Wiley's house. The proposed border line was the Sweet Springs and Fincastle Turnpike. Wiley and Shawver lived on the south side of the turnpike, and within the proposed new borders, while William Booth's tavern on the other side remained in Alleghany County.[47]

A similar controversy arose during an Alleghany and Monroe County survey conducted in 1856. In June, the Monroe County Court appointed James Vawter to complete a boundary survey of the jurisdiction: he finished his work in December. A geological error by the surveyor drew the border line from the peak of nearby Peters Mountain and cut off several miles of county territory to the northwest of Sweet Springs. The "Vawter Line" was only honored at the county level, although it was used in the 1870s as an accurate border survey for a new adjustment.[48]

Most petitions and memorials related to other local activities that needed state approval, such as some turnpike improvements or the establishment of a voting district. In February 1852, the General Assembly of Virginia was petitioned by virtually every Rich Patch Valley farmer to establish a voting precinct with a polling place at the Sugar Bottom Schoolhouse, which was situated close to the home of local political leader Colonel Madison Hook. Hook's public house was also close by.[49]

The establishment and location of polling places were sensitive issues. A new jurisdiction could affect the outcome of an election by wresting control from long-powerful local elites. Farmers had to travel great distances to vote, and eventually, as the population increased, the need for new polling places became apparent. The Potts Valley farmers in Alleghany County asked to have a new precinct established at the tavern of John Mastin. Their reasoning was sound.[50]

> ...in Time of high waters, your Petitioners, who are Citizens and Voters of and in said, County, are subjected to great Inconvenience in Consequence of having Dunlaps and Potts's Creek to cross repeatedly for the Distance of upwards of Twenty Miles...[51]

New power centers were created in the county. Alleghany County was slow to open new polling jurisdictions. By 1856, Robert Skeen's brick and timber hotel in Covington was one of eight polling places within the county. The sort of petition like the one above was usually granted, as it was in this case of the Mastin tavern. Memorials and petitions constituted the one tool of pure democracy the small mountain farmers had at their collective disposal. To be sure, local political motives lurked behind some. However, the object almost always was to benefit the group as a whole. It took an enlightened group of farmers to grasp and work the political process. Those who did not were led by those who did know the process. Judging by the numerous and varied petitions and memorials submitted over an extended period, it is likely most understood their political potential.[52]

The petitioners gained politicial rights at a price. Another political reality was the poll tax, a fee for the vote which kept many poor farmers away. When Alleghany County held its first elections in 1822, 534 men were subject to the measure. Although the amount varied, its existence depressed the number of voters.[53]

Local political offices were monopolized and used as steps to power. Voters in Alleghany County, which was formed in 1822, was served by just six county clerks prior to 1860. The first, Oliver Callaghan, was the son of tavern owner Dennis Callaghan. He left his clerkship in 1831 to become editor of the *Fincastle Democrat* newspaper. He was followed in turn by Andrew Hamilton, Beniah Hutchinson, and Johnson Reynolds. Andrew Fudge took over the clerkship and held it until 1858; he covered two elective offices during his clerkship. Lewis Holloway carried the office into the Civil War and later became editor of the *Covington Times*.[54]

Newspapers were an important part of the political process. It was part politics and part business. The 1823 *Fincastle Mirror* had four columns per page, the first with advertisements, lawsuit announcements, and foreign news. The second continued the foreign news, then switched to domestic issues. Political editorials with pseudonyms were popular. Two of them were the frequently-seen "Scribbler" or "Tom Scrawler." Marraige announcements were on page three. The last page contained some poetry as well.[55]

Typical of a political notation in the *Fincastle Mirror* was the "toast," printed in the paper from various locations to acknowledge public support for a candidate. Lewisburg's J. Bowyer Calwell was among ten Lewisburg citizens that toasted candidates on July 23, 1824. His choice for the presidency was Henry Clay, but not all toasts endorsed a candidate openly. Captain Cyrus Cary toasted, "The Presidential Candidate: may the successful one, imitate the example of Washington, and study well his valedictory address."[56]

The office of county justice in Alleghany County was occupied between 1822 and 1852 by multiple members of the same families. John and William Holloway both served, as did Potts Creek scions John and Michael Arritt. Three Persingers, two Skeens, two Hooks, two Damrons, and two Callaghans also served in the capacity of county justice. In Monroe County, four Hutchinsons served as county clerk from 1799 to 1865.[57]

Politics often affected and frustrated officeholders. County Clerk Oliver Callaghan wrote bitterly of his jurisdiction in the early days, but he did not specifically indicate a specific reason for leaving his clerkship. However, political life was heated, and his disenchantment may have involved the formation of the Whig Party. Oliver wrote on the subject to his brother William in Missouri in several letters. The first remarks were written from the Callaghans tavern in July 1833:

> Covington is getting more corrupt every day, an honest man
> has no business here. I would like for you to look out a situation
> for a store among wealthy settlers & where there is not
> much opposition & write to me on the subject as soon as
> convenient for I am determined on leaving here as soon as I can
> sell.[58]

A second letter was written to his brother William Callaghan the following summer that justified Oliver's decision to leave the area. His decision was based on a bigger mercantile market as well as distaste towards his former community.⁵⁹

> I have disolved my business with Steele & have opened a large store in Fincastle where I am doing much better than I did in this place. I have taken in Ferdinand Wiley as a partner, who has been managing the store for us, for the last 14 months & I find myself justified in leaving here [Callaghans] & moving to Fincastle.⁶⁰

Although the Alleghany County clerkship had been refilled several times, there was stability in the newly-formed county jurisdictions. Craig County was served by only two county clerks from its formation in 1851 to 1860. John W. Younger served for a year and then was replaced by Clifton G. Hill.⁶¹

Other coveted offices at the county level included those of justice and sheriff. The officeholders came from all walks of life, but most were popular in their home places, or the portion of the county they represented. Oren Morton chronicled the Monroe County jurors of 1820 to 1861, or the antebellum period. His 1852 listing included 28 men in seven districts, four elected from each. In Monroe, the sheriff was appointed until 1852. Morton noted that the work was performed by his deputies. However, either position of sheriff or deputy was a path to political power. Among those who chose this route was John W. Lanius, the first elected sheriff of Monroe, who had served as a deputy since 1849. Sheriffs in Alleghany included John Callaghan and Stephen Hook. County family dynasties were present in these offices as in others. Members of the Caperton, Dunlap, Alexander, and Erskine families served as deputies in Monroe.⁶²

Augustus A. Chapman, U. S. Senator and local businessman. (1803-1876). Courtesy: Peggy Thompson Steele.

Most other offices were specialized at both the national and local levels. The position of judge was unattainable to many, and those chosen often came from different areas. Those few who became state delegates or U.S. Congressman also served as representatives in some county capacity. William H. Terrill of Alleghany County served as state delegate from 1828 to 1831; he later had represented Bath County at an improvements convention. Augustus A. Chapman of Monroe served in the U.S. House of Representatives from 1843 to 1847; he also served as county militia leader.[63]

It cannot be denied that bottles and politics were two great interests that sometimes merged into one another. The ability to rise in politics and participate in the symbolic program of temperance was the key to antebellum politics in Alleghany and Monroe Counties. Churches had an early influential role in temperance and the development of role models in politics. Eventually, temperance organizations and political cooperation created tough alcohol laws. However, the family remained the best connection in determining most political aims. Many families had "dynasties" in county government and ceremonial roles. Even rise to higher national office was likely affected by elite family status as perceived by citizens of the county. However, county offices became frustrating to some. Elections were celebrations and prized highly. So when William Booth lost his tavern to drunkenness, he also lost any potential political status. The two interests were connected in this fashion.

Chapter 4.-New Gates: The Local Toll Road and the Emergence of Business Enterprise

One of the greatest enterprises of western Virginians from 1812 to 1860 was the construction of privately owned toll roads to facilitate access and commerce within the mountain terrain. This was a great achievement because resistance of eastern Virginia planters. By the 1820s the easterners feared losing representational and political power. They used legislative tactics to prevent much funding. For years, toll roads were limited to a few. The power of the planters was enough to limit new technology in transport, too. They effectively tied up the introduction of railroads in western Virginia to the 1850s, some 20 years. When it became obvious that the canal was to be continued west, a turnpike movement in western Virginia boomed in the mid-1840s. The canal plans fell short of its original goals, and for many years the turnpike was the primary type of transport improvement.

Many of the turnpikes or toll roads were originally Indian and buffalo trails. When white settlers came to the mountains, they simply used the same trails as bridle paths. A wagon road was built from Warm Springs to Lewisburg in 1782, and this good road undoubtedly fueled many efforts for a similar route in similar valleys to the south.[1]

Routes for establishing roads and delivery of mail were particularly important. Dennis Callaghan's tavern was an ideal postal hub. He was described as a small and jovial man. Originally an immigrant from Dublin, he arrived in the area about 1790. Callaghan quietly sensed the need for a tavern house and bought up large acreage. Callaghan was not quick to advocate his opinions to strangers on the subject of improvements to the mail route. When someone asked

Callaghan what his position was on an issue, the tavern keeper answered, "Mr. Stranger, I am exactly where you are."[2]

Callaghan knew his tavern made a profitable mail collection point. A few years after opening his tavern business in 1794, an official mail route opened between Staunton and Lewisburg. Callaghan may have had an official hand stamp to postmark incoming parcels, but no record is made of such an event. The stamp signified the importance of the tavern as an economic trade center with the trust of the National Government. By the late 1820s several postmasters received their stamps. James Calwell of the White Sulphur Springs had his delivered in 1829. The postmaster at Union received his in the mid-1830s.[3]

Early Improvement Movements

The Virginia Assembly was interested in promoting trade and easier transport of western Virginia's raw materials. In 1812, a commission was appointed to explore the headwaters of the James River to see how far boats could venture. The commission was chaired by Chief Justice of the Supreme Court John Marshall; several of his subordinates were James Breckinridge, William Lewis, James McDowell, William Caruthers, and Andrew Alexander. Although their findings were not conclusive, the commission's report wielded great influence in the passage by the Virginia Assembly of the Internal Improvements Act of February 5, 1816. The Virginia Department of Public Works was initiated.[4]

The period from February 1816 through 1830 was a lively one for western Virginia. News of impending plans for the James River & Kanawha Canal stirred up passions. A series of projects was rapidly introduced by anxious westerners or ambitious canal company businessmen who wanted to extend the canal as far as possible. However, there was a series of delays created by politicians who cared little for the project or its large expense. The Company drew many talented engineers and it cost dearly. Nearly $172,000 was spent on road improvements to improve transit between Covington and the Kanawha River.[5]

The delays caused some regional politicians to search for other means of funding improvements to keep up with a growing population. Recognizing private money took too long to raise, U.S. Congressman Ballard Smith of Lewisburg proposed an addition to the budget for the National Road, which stretched west from Cumberland, Maryland into Ohio. He wrote that the U.S. Government could subscribe two-fifths of the needed stock to a private company in Virginia for the purpose of developing transportation between the James River and the Kanawha River. The National Road was not germane to his home district, but Smith hoped for a further funding proposition. His proposal was not successful.[6]

Before the sectional opposition hardened to improvement projects, a full survey and map of western Virginia was undertaken. No real details were known about the lands to base decisions on future improvement. The Assembly had chosen to spend for initial roads into the mountains. The new Bureau of Public Works sent out engineers and cartographers to chart the areas in and around the Virginia mountains. Hugh Paul Taylor of Lewisburg, one of the surveyors, wrote:

In 1817 and 1818, I was engaged in Surveying for the New

Map of Virginia, -partly in execution of Andw. Alexander's two contracts, and of W.D.Merriweather's contract, with the Executive-in those parts of Virginia binding on, and near, the states of North Carolina, Tennessee, Kentucky, Ohio, and Maryland; and in most of those counties north of the James river, between the Allegany mountain and the Chesapeake bay-..[7]

The new map of Virginia, known as the Boye Map, was completed in large measure by Taylor's efforts in western Virginia.

Taylor stayed in the employ of the Board of Public Works until 1821, when he joined the James River Company as engineer. On the Board of Public Works that year, Taylor worked under John Wood in a detailed study of the Alleghany region. The result was an amazing feat of painstaking record collecting. Taylor and his cohorts detailed the ownership of homes in the myriad valleys and hollows. In the Potts Valley, between Blue Spring Run and the Sweet Springs stage road, only 16 houses were located, in family clusters on the 1821 Boye Map studies. The Virginia map was completed in 1827 after several such studies. Moses and John Persinger lived next to each other between Snake Run and Blue Spring Run. The only other house on the eastern bank of Potts Creek in this area was William Johnson's home. Three households of the Wolf family lived next to each other just north of the Sweet Springs stage road.[8]

The surveys were in progress by 1819-20, but the canal needed political support to make it a reality. The project found a vital ally in Virginia Governor Thomas Mann Randolph, the son-in-law of President Thomas Jefferson. On January 25, 1820, Randolph sent a recommendation to the House of Delegates to extend the canal from Lynchburg to Covington and to construct a road from there to the Kanawha River. Part of this effort was political. The Erie Canal, built under the leadership of New York Governor DeWitt Clinton, had no competition. The James River Company would undertake the Virginia project, which was watched with great eagerness by Virginia's elite.[9]

It was watched too closely. In 1827, the Virginia Legislature restricted the Baltimore and Ohio Railroad to service north of the Little Kanawha River, too far away for use by Alleghany County farmers and other businesses. Covington's elite took it as a slight and promptly petitioned the Virginia Assembly. The business leaders of Covington knew that the restriction was politically motivated. The investors in the James River Company, many of whom were prominent eastern planters or state officials, were not about to sanction competition for the James River & Kanawha Canal. Despite the loud protests of local western politicians, such as William Terrill and Hugh Paul Taylor, to repeal the measure, it fell upon deaf ears.[10]

> Your petitioners, inhabitants of the county of *Alleghany*, most respectfully beg leave to represent, that they have witnessed with equal surprise and regret, the policy adopted by the Legislature, in restricting the Baltimore and Ohio Rail-road Company to a route north of the Little Kanawha river. Your petitioners feeling a deep interest in every measure calculated to improve the condition of the Commonwealth, had long hoped to witness, on the part of Virginia, some effective exertions to sustain her relative rank with her sister states...[11]

Even later, the slow progress of western improvements was evident in speeches of local politicians. George Summers spoke at an 1851 statewide political gathering:

> My friends from Greenbrier and Monroe, in front of me, are still worse off, for they have no navigable river to lead them to other States when refused access to their own. They are landbound and mountain locked.[12]

The issue of internal improvements festered in western Virginia for years. In July 1828, a convention in Charlottesville had pushed for the completion of the canal, which had stopped. The incomplete Boye map series of western Virginia was just completed, and Claudius Crozet, a French engineer of excellent reputation, oversaw the canal plans to Covington. Several factors impeded further progress of a navigable canal, however. Past Covington the river was not conducive to canal traffic. A memorial was drafted during the 1828 convention for a road connection to the falls of the Kanawha River in order to continue the canal route to the Ohio River. However, the proposed cash outlay made the Assembly balk. A flurry of suggestions followed, including one for a stage line from Covington to Lewisburg, which was actually a necessity. Joseph Carrington Cabell, a longtime public servant and head of the canal, was stymied in most efforts to increase spending on the canal. Cabell's opposition to an all-railroad route and a fiscally conservative legislature led directly to the turnpike boom in western Virginia.[13]

The Turnpike Boom

The turnpike boom progressed in stages. In the years between 1828 and 1837, a number of major turnpike companies were incorporated. Among these were the Lewisburg and Blue Sulphur Springs, the Lexington and Covington, and the White and Salt Sulphur Springs. After the Panic of 1837, a financial crisis stemming from lax credit control in the many state banks, a new crop of companies appeared. The private road enterprises during this period were focused primarily on enhanced cross routes or secondary routes for convenience. Examples were the Rich Patch turnpike company and the Mountain Lake and Salt Sulphur Springs turnpike company.[14]

The efforts to continue the turnpike network through political and economic means continued for many years. Lewisburg hosted several conventions, the first in 1831. Covington held one in 1844. The meetings consisted mostly of local businessmen and politicians uniting over the issue of improvements. The meetings were short, usually two days. Committees were selected to draft the proceedings of the meeting and a draft of a memorial to be sent to the Virginia Legislature. Lewisburg's stone Presbyterian Church was used as the convention hall, and was graced with the active participation of the clergy to start the meetings. The conclusion was uniform: The legislature was asked to allocate money to continue the construction of the canal, which was constantly stalling, to Covington. There, a railroad line would be built to connect with the navigable portions of the Great Kanawha River. Several individuals proposed an all-railroad route directly from Richmond. The canal-rail plan was a goal of the James River & Kanawha Company from its reorganization in 1834, but financial strain and sectional tension blocked its implementation. The westerners would have to settle for improved roads.[15]

The condition of turnpikes in the region was, for the most part, deplorable. They were dusty, bumpy, and in most cases, they were little more than expanded trails. The Turnpike Act of February 1817 allowed for the state registration of private turnpike companies. The state could sell stock in a company once a certain percentage of capital stock was sold privately. The first turnpikes, which were used to access the springs, generated little profit; in fact, they were popularly called "summer roads."[16] Convention speeches, such as one given by George W. Summers in 1851, focused bitterly on the condition of major roads in western Virginia:

> We have a mud turnpike from Covington to the Ohio river, made on State account, and what is called an improved navigation of the Kanawha river, a work which has paid for itself many times over, in tolls exacted for its use.[17]

Even Henry Clay noted the bad roads to the springs during the later winter season. Typically muddy during the rainy and snowy period, he preferred to arrive from the north and the National Road rather than the harder direct routes.[18]

The roots of a new and privately-run toll road system was planted. Although direct routes to several private toll and stage roads were already firmly established, new grass roots pressure was applied after 1828 to expand the existing transportation system. Some of the older turnpikes were subdivided into several toll roads. Some hope was expressed that Senator Henry Clay's American System of nationally-funded improvements would assist the region and force the state to allocate money for improvements. However, President Andrew Jackson set precident by vetoing the Maysville Road project in Clay's home state of Kentucky in 1830. The proponents of improvements in western Virginia could no longer hope for eventual Federal support. They turned to conventions, like that in Staunton in 1831 to form a united political coalition. Private enterprise was found to be the only mechanism to achieve any reasonably fast internal improvement.[19]

Locally, John Shawver looked for improvement money from the Virginia Assembly. In his September 1835 memorial to the Assembly, Booth was concerned over the stretch of the Price's Mountain and Sweet Springs Turnpike that ran from Price's Mountain to the resort. No doubt Booth wanted to preserve his own tavern business, but he also disputed the sole ownership of the road by Jacob Price and his family.[20]

> That the former charter granted to Jacob Price and others will shortly expire. That the said Price and his family have had a monopoly of the said road for a number of years..frequently has been in bad repair, & probably has never been in such a state as it ought to have been considering the high rate of Tolls exacted for passing on the same.[21]

Price had been one of the original builders of the turnpike about 1809. The roads in the area were primarily Indian paths and rough trails, and its distinctive nature ensured a good profit in tolls. Booth called for state commissioners either to grade and repair the road or to create a state charter, reduce the toll charges, and pay the grading fees. The memorial was signed by local farmers and travelers alike. The non-locals among the 85 signatures were from Lynchburg, Bedford, and Farmville, Virginia, and from the state of Alabama. Although most of the signatures were those of individuals who lived near or along the turnpike, the broad base of support was deemed "reasonable" by the Assembly on December 14, 1835.[22]

Throughout much of his adult life, surveyor Hugh Paul Taylor was a tireless advocate of internal improvement in western Virginia. He had moved from Lewisburg to Covington. Taylor's interests went far beyond mapmaking. His attempts to improve transportation in Alleghany and Greenbrier Counties varied in tactics. He worked in public works and local law for years. As early as 1818, Taylor was working on a book to be called *Historical Sketches of the Internal Improvements of Virginia.* His writings were never printed in book form, but portions of the proposed book were published in various forms over the following twelve years. Most notable were long newspaper columns in the *Fincastle Mirror-Extra*. By 1829, Taylor was a tired revolutionary. He applied for the position of assistant engineer for the James River & Kanawha Company. As part of his application, Taylor included a three-page history of Virginia improvements in a letter to Delegate William Smith of Greenbrier, and he advised Smith that he considered the cost estimates quoted to the company on the Kanawha Falls extension to be high. Unfortunately, Smith was facing a fiscally conservative and cautious Assembly that did not want to chance a large improvements funding package on a mountain waterway. When Taylor died in January 1831, Covington lost its greatest and most knowledgeable champion of internal improvements. It was another decade before other western Virginians fully benefitted from Taylor's lobbying efforts.[23]

Care and operating capital of the local toll road fell to private shareholders. A group of citizens, most of whom lived close to the road in question, invested in the road, and some even maintained portions of it. Several local citizens were toll takers. As early as 1825, a tollgate existed at the tavern and postal facility of the Callaghan family. On the resort route of the Sweet Springs and Price's Mountain Turnpike near Potts Mountain, Andrew Wilson was one such caretaker. The Mountain House Tavern on the same stage road atop Potts Mountain was another. Tollgates could be very frequent depending on the turnpike company. Petitions and charters were filed with the Virginia Bureau of Public Works for each road. Most petition drives were headed by a local citizen of some means who lived close to the road. It was a good tactic, as it was necessary to convince the state that the road could be properly maintained.[24]

Tolltakers were sometimes innovated projects to create competition. A popular western Virginia tale involves a member of the Beirne family, probably Oliver, who financed the construction of a turnpike road from Sweet Springs because of a tollkeeper's actions. Beirne was irritated at the frequency of tolls on the road he was traveling. He approached a woman who collected the money. From his horse, Beirne threw a twenty-dollar bill onto the ground. The woman threw the change from his bill onto the same spot. Beirne decided a new road was preferable to a repeat performance of that incident.[25]

Western Virginia seemed destined to have a large-scale toll road system. The springs were popular with many out-of-state citizens, and since railroads and other means of transportation were limited in the area, the toll road reigned. This could mean a great deal of income during the peak vacation periods for the local farmer, the toll taker, and the springs owner. Advocacy of a large-scale transportation system was natural to western Virginia residents. The question arose to obtain the means of funding and maintenance of the needed stage roads to access the springs.

The maintenance of a stage or turnpike road involved a difficult and thankless routine. To drain the road properly from flooding due to frequent downpours, small ditches or furrows were dug at an angle into the roadbed to create water breaks. Water would funnel through the furrows and down the side of the road. To clear brush and debris from the road, drag chains were used. Maintenance was even more difficult close to a ford or major waterway.[26]

The ownership of most area roads was either private or semi-private. The Virginia Board of Public Works chartered many new companies composed of entrepreneurs and interested citizens. Annual reports were submitted to the state as well. There were many tollroads other than the Sweet Springs and Price's Mountain Turnpike. By the 1850s, area roads included those operated by the Fincastle and Covington Turnpike Company, the Sweet and Salt Sulphur Springs Turnpike Company, the Salem and New Castle Turnpike Company, and the Rich Patch Turnpike Company. These roads were destined for further improvements, such as the construction and maintenance of bridges.[27]

Bridges were essential to mountain roads. Some, such as Covington's Humpback Bridge, built in 1835, was covered. Others were placed at key points along stage roads to make an easier crossing of the regions many rivers and swollen creeks. In every case, bridges were expensive to maintain. The Panic of 1837, combined with natural disasters, impeded the progress of the James River & Kanawha Company's western plans. This was especially true in the Covington area, where the building of bridges virtually stopped.[28] In its 1839 annual report, the Board of Public Works explained the delay in progress:

> The heavy snows and great rise in western streams in March last, passed off without essential injury to any of the company's works. But, in addition to the completion of a portion of work left unfinished at the end of last year, the defects of the old masonry and the dilapidations of time, have rendered it unavoidable to incur an extroadinary expenditure in the renewal of bridges..This terminated the business of replacing the bridges over Howard's creek and over Dunlap's creek, which had been swept away by the flood of May 1837...[29]

The discouraging news did not stop attempts by western interests to obtain state aid to rebuild the damaged structures and further shield the local population from the tax burden imposed by almost constant repairs. Local citizens developed their own solutions. James Burk, the collector of tolls on the Covington Bridge, wrote second auditor John Brown in December 1838:

> The bridge is in a tolerably good condition now, except the floor. The planks have shrunk, and it will be necessary to have them placed closer, and consequently it will be necessary to procure some plank to fill up..The bridge

sustained considerable injury last May..I would respectfully suggest that if the board would take measures to exonerate the inhabitants of the county from paying toll, that I feel confident that the court would discontinue the road which passes around the bridge.[30]

The local businessmen had little trust invested in the Board of Public Works. James Byrnside of Monroe County felt that the legislators in Richmond opposed their interests. He wrote politician Felix G. Hansford:

I have very little confidence in in any app[lication] to the the board of Public Works. I may have done them injustice, but I did conclude when in Richmond the Board were more disposed to reward favourites [to] the Company or the public.[31]

Internal Organization: The Rich Patch Turnpike Company

The records and reports of the Rich Patch Turnpike Company provide insight into the organizational and social composition of such enterprises. Directors and president were appointed. A charter to the court and later the state was presented through attorneys. On August 18, 1837, the officers of the Rich Patch Turnpike Company presented its charter application papers to the county court at Covington. Samuel C. Robinson was president; the directors included iron magnate Edwin Jordan, Carleton Shirkey, local tobacco grower John King, and innkeeper Stephen Hook. A right of way was required by the courts to obtain the necessary land for the routes.[32]

Legal problems typically cropped up when land surveys were conducted. In order to open a public road like the one through the Rich Patch, a number of "disinterested" landowners were required to appoint commissioners in order to decide the reasonable need for the construction or the assessment of damages. In constructing the road, it pierced between tracts of Mary Herbert's land. It damaged some acreage of grazing land. Five landowners were chosen to assess the damage to Mary Herbert's land in 1837. The five were Snake Run area residents Samuel V. Gatewood, Achilles Dew, James Carson, William Carson, and Thomas E. Smith, the last four of whom surveyed a route and extolled the benefits of the road that September. The matter was dropped for some years. In 1852, the court allowed the next group of commissioners to resurvey the damaged areas. The lands of Mary Herbert, the owner of all the land on that part of the proposed byway, was then offered a price fairly assessed for the estimate damage. Mrs. Herbert sought a damage judgment of $47. The company argued that the increased land values equaled the amount of damages. The court found for Mrs. Herbert and awarded her $50 for loss of timber and ready access to parts of her own cropland. Even after Mrs. Herbert's death, the Rich Patch Turnpike Company petitioned to have the judgment set aside by Writ of Error. The petition was sent to the Circuit Court, but the company's petition was denied.[33]

The frustration in organizing fragmented interests for a toll road enterprise was evident. When preparing its progress report to the Virginia legislature, the Rich Patch Turnpike Company directors met at Roaring Run in December 1849. Colonel Edwin Jordan was appointed chairman of the company. The road was completed as far as Stephen Hook's house in the Rich Patch. A month later, the directors met at Hook's, at which time Stephen Hook was the new president pro tem of the company. The dominant figure in the enterprise was then Hook because the new section of road lay near his home interests. His son Madison Hook resigned his seat as State director in the Board of Directors of the Rich Patch Turnpike Company in October 1850, probably once the road was constructed past their holdings.[34]

Natural Resources

The economy of the region depended upon its natural resources. Agriculture, iron, timber, and spring waters, and agriculture were the most important components; everything else was based on these elements. Tourism developed from the springs. Iron and timber brought in transportation dollars. The agriculture and abundance of livestock brought reputation and new resident-farmers. As described earlier in the chapter, it is evident that the antebellum farmer of the Potts Valley took his business seriously.

Farming was a source of survival and pride. Unless a man came to the region with money or an existing business, farming was the starting point for most yeoman or common farmer. In this mountainous region, fertile land was at a premium. However, evidence showed that the farmers more than made up for it in the tending of livestock. Cows, sheep, and swine rambled in large field pens. The 1860 U.S. agricultural census showed that Alleghany farmers had particularly large herds. In the Rich Patch alone, John King had 5 horses, 3 milch cows, 3 cattle, and 32 swine worth $600. George M. Jameson had a modest 2 horses, 3 milch cows, 1 cattle, 7 sheep, and 15 swine. One of his Jameson's neighbors, Joseph Ervine, had 4 horses, 3 milch cows, 5 cattle, 12 sheep, and 23 swine. These were modest livestock holdings compared to those of the elite of the Rich Patch. Jesse Humphries had 11 horses, 7 milch cows, 14 cattle, 5 sheep, and 30 swine. Of course, Humphries did not live in the higher elevations, but on the fertile bottom land near a tavern establishment.[35]

Agricultural labor included the institution of slavery. The institution was not as widespread as in other sections of Virginia due to the mountainous terrain. The large landowner owned a few slaves on his acreage. Alleghany County farmers such as the Persingers kept small numbers of slaves. It was easier to escape into the hollows. A large number of hardscrabble, non-slaveowning farmers dominated the region. Many were unsympathetic to the institution, and there was risk of violence. In one case, Colonel John Persinger was stabbed to death by his slave, a man named Blue. The two had known each other a long time, but both men were intoxicated. In short, slavery assisted the elite farmers in a cursory fashion.[36]

The mining of iron ore became an important industry in the region. Early iron interests appeared on Dunlap Creek about 1800. In Wythe County a small-scale mining and furnace industry was operated by the Graham family. John Jordan and John Irvine came westward from Rockbridge County in 1827. Rich Patch and Potts Creek proved to be rich ore veins. The two men purchased vast acreage where they knew ore deposits could be located. The area that became known as Jordan Mines produced ore that was carted to local furnaces and forges, including Roaring Run, Lucy Salina, and Dolly Ann. Four charcoal furnaces were fully operational in the area by 1850. Together they could blast about 25-30 tons of pig iron in a week's time. The Jordan family opened Clifton Forge, a carriage ride from Covington, in 1828.

The Lucy Salina cold blast furnace farther east constructed by John Jordan's son Colonel Edwin Jordan and opened by 1830. Irvine's death in 1834 left the Jordans in control of the operation.[37]

Geologist W.B. Rogers performed early studies of the ore in the Alleghany County area. In an initial 1838 Virginia geological survey of resources in the state, Rogers verified what Jordan and Irvine already knew. The area was rich in iron, pyrite, and fossil rock. Rogers paid special attention to the Longdale ore near the Lucy Salina furnace and reported his finding in the 1838 annual report to the state. By doing so, Rogers indirectly fostered investment in the mountain counties.[38]

The problem of getting the ore to market, however, was a serious one. The ore had to be packed onto barges and taken to Richmond, and the process was often long and arduous, not to mention expensive. The economic risks taken by Jordan and Irvine were considerable compared to other iron interests working east of the mountains, but the supply of ore proved more than the trouble of digging it once its transportation options improved.[39]

The making of small household manufactures, such as crafts or hand tools and small-scale industry, could thrive if a reputation for quality was attained. William Madison Bostic of Monroe County started making furniture about 1845 after serving an apprenticeship under Jackson Cadle of Union. The furniture became regionally distinctive, but its manufacture was a difficult business in an area with little cash. Bostic accepted food in place of cash at times. Lewisburg furniture maker Thomas Henning, who married into a local family, made distinctive cabinets, desks, and chairs. In 1812, James Calwell used Henning's chairs at White Sulphur Springs. The popularity of pottery and ceramics reached a apex under the skilled hands of George Newman Fulton. Fulton began his pottery works in a shop along the Richmond & Fredericksburg road and soon moved to Potts Creek. His great contribution to western Virginia social life was a 20-gallon water cooler dated May 1856. It was decorated with an American Eagle design in blue salt glaze and was used at John Crow's tavern. Fulton reportedly had a kiln with enough space for 1,000 pounds of clay; his stoneware was signed near a painted flower design. His many ceramic pieces continue to sustain incredible popularity. A Virginia study has confirmed that Fulton's kiln at Potts Creek was in full operation from 1867 to 1875, although the Crow cistern proved his presence in the area prior to 1860. Fulton moved to a new kiln near Fincastle sometime after 1880.[40]

The mountains supplied fuel for local industry and existing transport systems until the completion of the Covington & Ohio railroad, which would then furnish a supply of coal in the railroad. The lumber of Alleghany needed a cheap mode of bulk transit or the fuels would remain undisturbed for many years. Limestone and hydraulic cement abound with wood and water sufficient to make them useful.[41]

Thompson McAllister was a relative stranger to western Virginia when he arrived in Covington in December 1849. The Pennsylvania native was a Henry Clay Whig with an enterprising outlook towards the area's natural resources and potential. He bought 2,200 acres near Covington as well as flour mills within the town. However, McAllister was not content to rest at this. He saw the potential of reaching the timber and iron resources of the region by way of railroad, which for some twenty years had been kept out of the area. Construction of the Covington & Ohio Railroad was underway in the early 1850s.

Fulton Stoneware. Courtesy: Helen Baker.
Photograph by Glenn Vogel.

McAllister clamored for its completion.[42]

Despite pleas for a cheap transportation, it took a full participation of the key members of the Richmond delegation with the state legislature to make it a reality. In order to gather the needed support, a large convention was held at White Sulphur Springs in August 1854 to promote the speedy construction of the railroad from Covington to Ohio. The issue attracted some well-known personalities from around the state. William Cabell Rives, Andrew Stevenson, and John Minor Botts were all representatives of their respective counties. Regional leaders that attended included Thompson McAllister, Charles Callaghan, Andrew Fudge, Samuel Price, and Allen Taylor Caperton. Rousing speeches were given by Rives and Joseph Segar of the eastern shore. Rives wanted a convention concerning more generalized improvements meetings in several months time. Botts gave an address that was followed by a speech from the governor of Virginia. The convention lasted three days.[43]

The significance of the White Sulphur Convention was enormous. It was the first single Virginia improvements convention to have widespread representation. After years of unanswered petitions, the White Sulphur Convention achieved a multi-sectional agreement to give western Virginia-and Covington specifically-a new industry. Even the leading politicians had to acknowledge the advantages of trade in a rail line from Covington to Ohio. Segar's speech was printed for mass circulation after Rives turned down a chance to have his words memorialized. Supporting documentation was added to the printed proceedings to further validate the importance of the issue. Benefits were compared to costs. The proposed 150 miles of the Covington & Ohio Railroad would cost $10.5 million.[44]

Amazingly the western Virginia railroad was slower to develop than many other areas of the state. It must be remembered that by 1854, the railroad was already 30 years old. Virginia lagged far behind in its technology due to sectional and political strains during the Jacksonian period. The canal was a traditional source of pride to Virginians, and they were slow to move to the newer railroad. The White Sulphur Convention alone did not get the James River & Kanawha Canal to the Covington area. It took another governor, Henry Wise, to actually wrest the money from the legislature. By 1860, the canal was almost complete.[45]

Improved methods of travel indirectly helped others in starting businesses, particular those who manned tollgates and kept taverns. The roads to the springs were dotted with small taverns, inns, and ordinaries. The stage road to Sweet Springs had several within close proximity. Scott's Tavern, built about 1825, was on the eastern base of Potts Mountain. Originally the tavern was simply several adjoined log cabins. The tavern itself had a total of six rooms for weary travelers. William Scott and his wife, a relative of Jacob Price, ran their tavern house for decades. When William Scott died in 1854, his widow continued the operation of the establishment into the Civil War.[46]

The Mountain House, which was run by the Walker Family, stood a few miles at the top of the mountain. On the mountain's western base stood the Booth and Shawver Taverns.[47] A later resident of the old Booth Tavern, Pullen Sizer, described the intricate construction of the house.

The house had been built of virgin timbers, chestnut and white oak logs, mortised at junction and with visable hewn hashmarks throughout. The inside was done with lathes made of white oak nailed in place with blacksmith shop nails. Plastering consisted of sand, lime and animal hair. In our day we wallpapered over much of the plaster. It had a huge attic and the rafters were five inches square joined with one, one half-inch hewn yellow locust pins.[48]

Another establishment was the Stringer Tavern. Its Proprietor, John Stringer, knew his ordinary was secluded enough to attract overnight guests who ventured between Sweet and White Sulphur Springs. His private thoroughfare was used by stagehands and further enhanced his prospects.[49]

In Alleghany County, there was no lack of taverns. the first tavern license was issued to Fleming Keyser. Along the Sweet Springs-White Sulphur-Covington road was the Callaghan Tavern and also that of Colonel John Crow at the halfway point. Crow was a colorful figure, who, like Dennis Callaghan, was the stuff of folk legend. Blanche Bess wrote in 1941, "It was well know that old John was a "Go-getter," and slept with one eye open, on the lookout for business for the tavern and the mill."[50]

The location and popular stories enhanced Crow's business, which was in existence at the time of the formation of Alleghany County in 1822. In fact the trail between Crow's Tavern and White Sulphur Springs was known as "breaking the backbone" of the mountains. Many picnics gathered around the tavern, which filled its porch areas, or "dog alleys", with many visitors seeking entertainment. A confirmed tale referred to Crow's pet bear, Bruin, which he rode in races.

President Martin Van Buren, who was a good friend to Monroe County resident Andrew Beirne, made the long horse ride from the springs to dine at Colonel Crow's house. The establishment was of great comfort to a traveler and had a fireplace in every room and heavy doors lined with pegs to keep out the cold. Originally two rooms, it was later expanded to eighteen. A hot meal could be eaten for twelve cents and a single bed for just under nine cents.[51]

The comforts of the tavern changed as its clientele grew. Even Dennis Callaghan's tavern house began as a primitive and small structure. Cut logs were used to build the structure, but stone was used to create permanency. The innkeeper expanded his structures and services as traffic increased. Before Callaghan's death, around 1820, permanent quarters were built for both slaves and livestock. Family members assisted in the entertainment of guests by playing musical instruments.[52]

The ironworkers had their tavern as well. Close to Jordan's holdings at Longdale was the Armentrout Tavern, a brick building on the turnpike between Lexington and Covington. George Armentrout, the original owner, ran the facility from 1824 until his death in June 1839. His son John took it over before selling it after the Civil War. The lack of competition along the Covington and Lexington road enabled the tavern to last.[53]

The mystique and comforts of the antebellum tavern have continued to fascinate readers in stories of its visitors and keepers. The reality was that competition was heavy along some routes and sparse on other roads. Sometimes attracting business by unconventional means was necessary. The area stage roads were long and often required several days or weeks to reach a destination. These taverns doubled as inns and could be quite lucrative.

Tavern keep, springs owner, farmer, and canal construction worker were dependent upon each other to survive and to profit. Each had an important part of the frontier economy. The western Virginian worked with what resources were available, using the natural advantages of the region to its fullest potential. The frontiersmen attempted to create new avenues of business through the springs and a wider transport system in such a way.

Chapter 5.-The Farmer-Soldier Communities in Wartime, 1812-15 and 1845-48

The wars against Britain and Mexico were opportunities to the western Virginian. It was for the spirited and adventurous, but of course death was all too common in war. Much of it occurred from disease in marshy or hot environments rather than gunpowder. The image of the brave frontiersman was an important part of folklore to their descendants. Stories had been passed from father to son about the Battle of Point Pleasant, where local men from Greenbrier, Monroe, and Botetourt Counties fought against the Shawnees under their chief, Cornstalk, in 1774; about the victories of hard-bitten soldiers under George Rogers Clark during the Revolutionary War; mountaineers holding their own against the British on the slope of King's Mountain. There was undeniable pride in wearing the military insignia or attire of their local unit.[1]

The War of 1812

The pride was echoed in the local units that were mustered during the War of 1812. The region's men served in many scattered units, but Captain Andrew Nickell's company of the 4th Virginia Militia Regiment included the largest complement of them. Nickell himself was a Monroe County resident whose forebears had fought at Point Pleasant. The members of the unit hailed from many western Virginia counties, plus Buckingham County near Richmond. Among other assignments, Captain Nickell had to bring his troops to the disease-ridden Craney Island near Norfolk to help guard the mouth of the

Hampton Roads waterway in late 1814. There had been a battle on the island the previous year, but since then, only mosquitoes in large quantities resided there. The unhealthy nature of the expedition claimed many lives from disease.[2]

Among the farmers from the region who served in Nickell's company were William Cornwell, Nathan Bush, Joseph and William Dunsmore, James N. Linton, Daniel Jarvis, John Patton, Elijah and Robert Pritt, Matthew Rayhill, and Robert and Thomas Wylie. While most of these men were Monroe County yeoman from the Gap Mills region, Linton and several others were from the Potts Creek region. For their service they were paid eight dollars a month. Nickell's unit came out of the war essentially intact. Their pride came mainly from wearing the uniform, especially since very few of Nickell's men ever saw a British soldier.[3]

A greater source of pride was the soldier's status within the frontier community. Their descendants would later decorate many of their soldier-ancestors' graves with war markers or notations of service. Area counties sent in their troops. Monroe County scion Andrew Beirne became a captain of a militia unit. Greenbrier County's 79th Virginia Regiment marched to the Ohio River under Lewisburg resident James W. Mathews. They reached the Midwest before turning back in the spring of 1813.[4]

A sidelight of the area's commitment to the American cause in the War of 1812 was the naming of the town of Covington. When engineers for the James & Kanawha Canal explored the area, they reached the furthest point of navigation on the Jackson River. They called the area "Mouth of Dunlap," for the tributary creek nearby. After American Brigadier General Leonard Covington was killed on

November 11, 1813, on Lake Ontario, no fewer than 20 towns and counties were named for him; one of these was Mouth of Dunlap.[5]

The War of 1812 troops were recruited heavily in the area and many men volunteered to serve. There was little actual contact with the British by those who volunteered. In fact, no military event ever occurred in the region. By the time most units were mustered from western Virginia, the war was almost over. In January 1815, the Battle of New Orleans was the decisive victory the Americans needed to end all hostilities.[6]

According to records of the time, other local citizens also saw military service. One was Jacob Tingler, who served in the 4th regiment under the militia company of Captain John Pitzer. Most of his company was raised in the Potts Creek area. His widow, in her request for his service pension, claimed that Tingler had been drafted in Botetourt County on August 22, 1814, and had served about six months. He served at Norfolk until the expiration of his service in February 1815. Joseph Ervine, who was a small boy at the time of Tingler's service, signed as an attesting witness.[7]

The thirty years between the War of 1812 and the Mexican War were patriotic ones. Many of the local farmers were involved in the local militia. However, their meetings were somewhat more social than military; there were no enemies to fight. Two musters occurred in April and October. For these events, the officers of the 108th Militia of Monroe County wore the old tri-corner hats of the colonial era. The company would gather at the Royal Oak in Union, but they did little drilling and none with arms.[8]

Colors (battle flags) were essential to define a regiment. In 1833, Colonel John Crow of Alleghany's 128th Virginia Regiment, 13th

Brigade, petitioned for monies promised for the battalion colors to be used in musters and ceremonies. Joseph Ervine was first lieutenant of the regiment in April 1843 and captain of riflemen in December 1844. His commissions were issued by Samuel Carpenter and signed by Virginia Governor James McDowell.[9]

Pride in military service of the western Virginians of this era reflected in official records as well as exstant mementos. The relative strength of the local militia was reported to the Virginia General Assembly in that body's annual Senate Journals. The brigade membership return lists of 1843 reveal that Monroe County had 1,287 men in the 108th Militia, compared to the eastern Virginia regiment, Westmoreland County's 111th, which had only 546 men in it. The numbers were consistent in both eastern and western Virginia when comparing county troop participation in the war.[10]

The Mexican War offered an opportunity for the area's next generation of men to distinguish themselves. By then the militia was not a prominent unit. Rather most of the local units were consolidated into national companies. Many of the region's men enlisted in Company K, U.S. Volunteers, or Voltiguers. This company mustered its officers at White Sulphur Springs in Greenbrier County under the command of Captain James H. Calwell. The captain was a West Point graduate and the son of the White Sulphur's owner. Among the company's local complement were Hiram Baker and George W. Craft of Alleghany County, and Reuben Ball and Larkin Thompson of Monroe. The company also included men from other Virginia counties such as Albemarle. After raising his company, Calwell's men were assigned to the command of General Zachary Taylor. The pension records of Hiram Baker note that they marched to Jalapa, Pueblo, Vera

Cruz, and Mexico City. Calwell did not survive; he was killed leading his men at the Battle of Vera Cruz on February 23, 1847. The remainder of his unit served about 60 days under the Mississippi Rifles of Colonel Andrews. Those soldiers who survived sailed to Fort McHenry in Baltimore for discharge. The members of Calwell's company are listed in Appendix B.[11]

Other regional scions of elite families led military units in the Mexican War. James Francis Preston was captain of 1st Regiment, Virginia Volunteers. This unit was raised in late 1846 and served the balance of the war. Sixty-year-old Captain Henry Erskine went to Mexico as a quartermaster. With his experience in the mercantile business, it was a suitable task. However, Erskine could not adjust to the hot Mexican environment. He died of dysentery on September 26, 1847, near Monterey.[12]

The local newspapers furnished to the local farmers what little information could be learned about this far-away fight. Papers from towns like Lewisburg and Fincastle could be obtained, but accurate and timely reporting was hard to come by, due to the great distances involved. However, the war was followed with great interest throughout the South, including western Virginia.

The farmer-soldier of 1848 was to serve in war one last time. The opening days of the American Civil War saw area militia units serve the Confederacy, but the militia here proved obsolete, except where it provided local security. The large armies required full-time participation, and the old revolutionary image of the minuteman dropping his hoe for the rifle became a thing of the past.

For the entire antebellum period, however, the farmer-soldier was to its contemporary citizen that revered minuteman. In 1840, William

Henry Harrison, for instance, was known as much a military figure as a farmer; the presidential candidate running as a patriotic farmer at the plow. The farmers of Alleghany and Monroe served as farmer-soldiers until the lifestyle became unwieldy.[13]

6.-The Religious Community in Western Virginia

Religion was a binding force in the antebellum communities of western Virginia and elsewhere. It kept people united in a Darwinist society where the weak often succumbed to misfortune or death. Receptivity to religion was cyclical in nature. When lone frontiersman first ventured into the backwoods of Virginia, religious freedom might have been the factor that drove their action. Some felt far from religious restraint in the cold mountains. By the 1820s, however, a Protestant revival appeared to have spread among the people of the mountain counties.

In the 1780s, religious freedom in the region was a real issue. Most residents of Virginia worshiped in the Episcopal faith, the American branch of the old British Anglican religion. The exception was western Virginia. The denominations and sects which departed too far from the Episcopal core were violently reproached. The severe treatment of Baptists in Culpeper County was just one example. The Baptists were persecuted there by law and summarily imprisoned in the early 1770s because of their religion. Even James Madison was appalled by the treatment of the Baptists.[1]

Scotch-Irish of the area were more tolerant of some of the sects that arrived. Some even helped despite their differences. Edward Keenan was a Catholic of Scottish background who donated land to build the Methodist hub of Rehoboth Church in 1784. Germans founded pockets of new settlements along the creeks in Alleghany County. Competition with the Presbyterian religion existed, but it remained the dominant religion for some years and maintained a constant identity.[2]

The reason for the religious tolerance was primarily due to James

Madison's statute mandating religious freedom in the Commonwealth of Virginia. In the mid-1780's, religious toleration became a law, which stripped the Episcopal faith of its former status as the state religion. Much of Virginia was slow to change its religious ways, however.[3]

The Presbyterians also had strong personalities as ministers. The Reverend John McElhenney presided over the Presbyterian bastion in Lewisburg. Born in South Carolina in 1781, he began studies at Yale and completed them at Washington College in Lexington, Virginia. The Lexington Presbytery sent him to Greenbrier and Monroe Counties in 1808. He officially became pastor of the Presbyterian churches at both Lewisburg and Union, and remained at this dual post until Reverend David R. Preston took over the religious duties at Union in 1834. His circuit took him to Gap Mills in Monroe County and the house of William Haynes. The following week saw McElhenney preaching a sermon at the Monroe County Courthouse. On these weekends he would stay with Andrew Beirne or the Alexander family in Union. He did not easily surrender his duties at the courthouse. McElhenney stated to his granddaughter Rose Fry that, "it was no small trial to my feelings to sever the connection which had existed for so many years, and to give up a people to whom I felt bound by so many ties..."[4]

Under McElhenney's energetic efforts, small churches dotted the countryside and made their way into the narrow valleys. McElhenney presided over the beautiful stone Presbyterian church in the center of Lewisburg and later over the Lewisburg Academy, which adjoined its property. Within the church McElhenney addressed the Lewisburg Internal Improvement Convention in 1831 held there, only a year after new additions had been made to greatly increase its size. Along with Andrew B. Davidson, McElhenney served as an official Presbyterian representative during the designation of Covington as a separate jurisdictional seat in 1819. Neither McElhenney nor Davidson was a permanent resident of Covington, so many congregational services were led by the elders of the church. The first elders were Conrad Fudge, Peter Wright, and John Brennemer.[5]

South of Covington, Rich Patch Valley was a vital stronghold of Presbyterian faith. Wealthy citizens ensured the rise of the church by their land and monetary donations. The helpful support of Captain Henry Massie, who married Susan Preston Lewis of Sweet Springs in 1810 and moved to 3,000 acres in the nearby Falling Springs Valley, contributed to the success of the Falling Springs Presbyterian Church. The success of that church centered around the Houston family. Preacher Samuel Houston and his son Samuel Rutherford Houston were actively involved with the religious community. The younger Houston eventually settled with a congregation in the town of Union.[6]

The attendees at an 1843 meeting at New Castle organized the Montgomery Presbytery from most counties in that region of Virginia. Despite its recent jurisdictional arrangement, the Presbyterian Church in that vicinity slowed in growth in comparison to other denominations in the area. The old Scottish church appeared to have a solid following, but the area was subject to newfound religious exposure which diminished its overall membership.[7]

The Methodists made early inroads into the region. Bishop Francis Asbury visited Rehoboth and the springs area; journal entries from his 1790 visit show the significance of the Potts Creek area to the Methodists.

Friday, 9.[July] We had a tedious, tiresome journey over hills and mountains to Potts Creek. After a melting season at brother Joseph Carpenter's, we came to brother James Wright's, where we were informed of the death of dear brother John Tunnell.
Saturday, 10. Brother Tunnell's corpse was brought to Dew's chapel.[8]

The religion centered around mass conversions and meetings known as revivals or camp meetings. Rehoboth, the first Methodist church to be established west of the Alleghany Mountains, was a medium-sized log structure, a total of 22 by 29 feet. Its chief construction engineer was Revolutionary War veteran Samuel Clark.[9]

Rehoboth became a rallying point for Methodist missionaries. Like Asbury, however, the missionaries were itinerants and moved on to spread their doctrine. From 1812 to 1821, ten pastors served at Rehoboth. The transient nature of the missions was not conducive to active upkeep of the church. By 1831 Rehoboth church was badly run down, all of the glass nearly gone. Accounts like this embarrassed the church. To bring back Rehoboth, scheduled events included an 1842 revival at the church. This one event converted 100 people.[10]

For the Methodist faith, 1844-45 was a pivotal time. The church and distinctive doctrines split along northern and southern regional lines. Lewisburg, under the influence of the writings of Southerner Sam Black, reflected much of the opinion of the region. A choice had to be made by the mountain populace between the northern and southern views of the church. The area fell within the boundaries of the Baltimore Conference. William Taylor, called "California Bill" and the nephew of Hugh Paul Taylor of Covington, was an active itinerant minister in the area by March 1845. The itinerant's committment had an impact on the community at large. Jake Wickline and his wife deeded for one dollar the property that became the Cokesbury Church. Many small Methodist chapels were formed in this way by the local citizens themselves.[11]

Joseph Pinnell, who was born in 1767, was an itinerant preacher before settling in the Potts Creek area. His long term of service and friendship with Francis Asbury inspired the choice of location for the 1857 revival meeting by the Reverend Brillhart. Brillhart was a Southern Methodist with no church of his own, but great plans to have a great camp meeting to create mass conversions. Local resident Jake Johnson opened his home for the meeting to Brillhart in the dead of winter. Potts Creek was iced over, and people came in sleighs over the creek and attended in droves.[12]

Shortly after the meeting, Mrs. Pinnell donated land along Potts Creek for a permanent Methodist structure; the original Pinnell's Chapel was built about 1860. Not far from Pinnell's Chapel were Shoaf's Methodist Chapel, which dated from 1853, and Wolfe's Chapel, which dated from 1850. The propensity to built many permanent structures on the sites of former revivals, such as Pinnell's, highlighted the success of such gatherings.[13]

Many Germans relocated from the Shenandoah Valley and brought the Germanic Brethren faith into the Potts Creek area. Early German-American ministers who presided in the Potts Creek Valley and the Rich Patch by 1860 included B.F. Moomaw, Peter Nininger, and George M. Jamison preached in the Potts Creek Valley and the Rich Patch by 1860. The Germanic Brethren enjoyed wide popularity after the Methodist revival period waned.[14]

Baptists tended not to settle in areas already established by other dominant religious areas. They prevailed in small settlements in Southwest Virginia; Wythe and Montgomery Counties had many Baptist and Pietist communities. The fundamentalist Baptists made their way with more strength into what is now Craig County.

New Castle was heavily influenced by a primitivist group led by Pennsylvanian Alexander Campbell. The Campbellites, as they were eventually called, were inspired by a Shaker-like church that shunned much of the traditional Baptist doctrine. Giles County resident Landon Duncan had gathered a congregation of "primitive Christians" near Sinking Creek. By 1828, many traveling preachers of the new faith, such as Joseph Thomas and William Lane, had visited Sinking Creek and inspiration to spread this new doctrine. Thomas, known as the "great white pilgrim" because of his long white robes, personally baptized many local residents. The group generally followed the religious doctrine of Alexander Campbell; they founded the Disciples of Christ, or Christian Church. This new group appeared to reject the traditional Baptist doctrine in favor of a looser hierarchy. Thomas's and Dr. Chester Bullard's lasting influence on the New Castle vicinity inspired the construction of the Gravel Hill Church in that area. Covington had a similar personality in William Hughart.[15]

The Baptists did gain strength in Monroe County. Near the Greenbrier County line, a group swelled from a small core of twelve in the 1780s. Under the leadership of John Alderson Jr., the Old Greenbrier Church was organized. By 1801, the small church became part of the Greenbrier Association. In 1812 the Association had a total of a dozen churches with 339 members. The Indian Creek Primitive

Church was also organized by Alderson in 1792. The Sinks Grove and Peterstown churches, close to areas organized by Baptists in Monroe County, started up by 1846. The Baptists started a church in the Sweet Springs Valley in 1859.[16]

If the Baptists had trouble achieving an early foothold in the area, Catholicism had more difficulty. Until Father John Walters arrived, few Catholics lived in the Sweet Springs Valley. Father John, who became the first pastor at the Church of St. John the Baptist in 1850, was the first resident priest in the area; he covered four counties in his parish. He had to travel long distances to perform his duties, including several journeys to Longdale to baptize ironworkers' children.[17]

A single church outside Covington, known as Mount Carmen, had been erected in 1822. There were still many scattered Catholic families then living in Alleghany County, according to Reverend Victor C. LeClerq, an author of a booklet on the subject in the early 1980s. Many of these were immigrant Irish families who worked on the mines and roads in the area. A few German Catholics arrived fresh from the European political strife of the late 1840s. Pockets of mostly German Catholics remained in the area throughout the antebellum period.[18]

The Virginia springs were visited by ministers of many faiths. The Reverend James Madison was one of the first to analyze the healing waters. The cousin of the president was a frequent lodger in the Sweet Springs area. One of the most eccentric and fascinating clergymen of all, Methodist itinerant preacher Lorenzo Dow, made his appearance in the area several times. A prolific writer and a circuit rider, Dow had inspired mass conversions by his fiery speeches. Largely printed on one of his many tracts was the title. "How to Curse and Swear, LIE, CHEAT AND KILL, according to law!"[19]

The life of the itinerant preacher required a tough and flamboyant personality. On his way to Clinch Valley in southwest Virginia, Dow stopped at Fincastle in on both his 1803 and 1805 circuits. As in the case of many itinerant preachers, the mileage took its toll on his horses and clothing. In April 1805, Dow asked Fincastle residents for money to pay for new horseshoes from a local blacksmith. Not long after, he became too sick to keep up his circuit duties and went into semi-retirement.[20]

Despite the occasional colorful personality, the area was settled primarily by Scotch-Irish Presbyterians and German Pietists. Methodist and Baptist missionaries also arrived, and mass conversions were conducted by itinerant ministers and at camp meetings. By 1860, many different religions were practiced in the area. Although Methodists, Presbyterians, and Baptists dominated the population, minority religion was highly tolerated. Liberal toleration could be traced to the 1780s settlement of the area, when many had to flee the Episcopal majority in the east for greater right of religious practice in the mountains.

7.-Educating the Populace

The need for education was recognized early by the settlers in the area. Before 1810, farmers organized and funded the education of their children. These institutions were known as pay schools, because many of the instructors were transient and set up temporary schools in the dormant old fields of farmers. Unfortunately, many farmers could not afford the required funds for this type of schooling, but the "old field" system was known to have benefited the children of area businessmen. Dennis Callaghan's sons and daughters attended a subscription or pay school run by Presbyterian schoolmaster Francis Crutchfield. Crutchfield operated his school close to the Callaghan's tavern and maintained a longtime friendship with William Callaghan, one of the innkeeper's eldest sons who later became a teacher himself.[1]

Virginia was fortunate enough to have two early governors interested in education, John Tyler, Sr., and James Barbour. Barbour, who served from 1811 to 1814, was influential in creating the General Literary Fund of Virginia, which provided a county school commission system for educating children. This was particularly important in educating the poor farmers' children of the western Virginia counties. The commissioners of each county were required to file annual accountings with the state of each pupil's name and age in order to obtain money from the Literary Fund. Teachers also had to list the number of students and the days on which they taught.[2]

The Literary Fund was tracked carefully by Virginia state officials. Although reports were kept by the second auditor, officials of even higher rank were concerned about the continued success of the fund. On December 30, 1825, Greenbrier County officials met with

Governor Tyler and Lieutenant Governor Peter Daniel. The good reputation of the Literary Fund was reflected in governor's messages over the entire period.[3]

While state officials kept close financial ties to the fund, the money had to be tightly justified and documented; many forms were to be sent to the second auditor. These reports were strictly monitored by officials and caused considerable confusion. Alleghany County officials were angry over both the length and complex nature of the forms.[4]

Schools were generally founded under primitive conditions. The first schoolhouses were crude structures. The community that became Paint Bank built its schoolhouse-a log structure-about 1845. The conditions inside these institutions were little better than out. Some only had crude benches to sit on.[5]

Schools connected with various churches became popular in the mid-1800s. Sunday schools-a Baptist innovation-became as popular; by 1853, the Baptists noted the existence of 20 such schools and 140 teachers in Greenbrier County. Earlier, Reverend John McElhenney's Lewisburg Academy had been chartered by the Virginia Legislature in January 1812 as a center of Presbyterian learning. McElhenney was the primary teacher until 1827. William E. Withrow stressed the importance of the Reverend's emphasis on higher emphasis.[6]

> My first connection with the academy lasted from 1816 to 1828. During this period Mr. McElhenney manifested an unceasing interest in the institution and everything connected with it. The school aspired to be an Academy for fitting young for College. Besides the regular English branches, advanced mathematics and the Latin and Greek languages were taught.[7]

McElhenney organized his academy to be a preparatory school for advanced secular and religious studies; he geared his courses towards entry into the colleges of the time. McElhenney noted in 1858:

> Many of them [the pupils] have been and still are eminently useful as ministers of the Gospel, physicians and lawyers, and very many others are filling, with credit to themselves and usefulness to their fellow-men, other stations in society.[8]

Most of the books used during this period were rather basic. The early old field schools had many historical and literary works to study. The Callaghan children read Mason Weems's *Life of Washington*, Lord Chesterfield's *Principles of Politeness*, and Francis Crutchfield's 1800 text on English grammar. Law and poetry books were likely to have been read; the Callaghan children wrote on both topics. In 1834, the Alleghany County book list included *Webster's Spelling Book*, *Pike's Arithmetic*, and the *New York Reader*. Other books, such as the *American Primer* and *Adam's Geographies*, were added by 1838.[9]

Increasing school participation in farming communities was a slow process. Some families were too poor to afford the time. Counties in western Virginia adopted a commission system each at its own pace. In 1840, prior to the creation of an official educational board in Alleghany County, 776 children were eligible to attend school. The five Literary Fund-supported facilities had only 88 children. Three years later a county board was initiated. The Board consisted of Joseph and Andrew Damron, Charles King, John McD.Mann, Alexander Rayhill, Sampson Sawyers, Henry Smith, Isaac Stull, and James Warren. Thirteen schools were then in operation. Alleghany County received $243.33 for their school expenses in 1843. In Monroe County, trustees also occupied the positions of commissioners. When the state turned to a standardized district reporting system about 1846, Monroe County used primarily the older version of county scoring for a few years longer. The district assignments that teachers received looked on paper as if they were following a bounded deed plat. Their districts followed long and sometimes lengthy assignment or "lines" along landmarks as deeds often stated.[10]

> Lewis S. Reynolds is appointed for District No. 11 which is bounded as follows: Commencing at the hanging rock then with the line of No. 10 to the top of Caldwell's Mountain, thence up said mountain with No. 9 to the Roanoke line; thence with the Roanoke line to the Giles line, thence with the Giles line to the Monroe line and thence with the Monroe line to the Beginning.[11]

The district system eventually prevailed over county scoring. In the Potts Creek Valley, many children went to the successful District Number 8. During the years of 1848-49, teacher George W. Carpenter educated six Arthur children and three Linton children. In 1853, James F. Bean taught five Jarvis and five Lawhorn children. That same year, Henry A. Walker taught three Wiseman children.[12]

The teachers of District eight were mostly men, but a few women also taught during the pre-Civil War period. During the period 1851-52, John H. McNutt served as the district commissioner. His teachers included Henry C. Damron, Chapman J. Cale, Martha Crosier, George W. Carpenter, Wellington Hawkins, William R. Stringer, and

James F. Pugh, James F. Bean, Martha A. Walker, and John Watson. This trend would change during the war.[13]

The period from 1812 to 1860 saw a marked rise in the mass spreading and teaching of primary educational skills. Poor farm children found access to a better way of living through the state's Literary Fund. Although the fund had bureaucratic drawbacks, there was little doubt its benefits were considerable. Counties gradually were divided into school districts as the population increased. Schools and books improved as 1860 approached. With the work needed to spur economic prosperity in the mountains, education was necessary to advance.

Genealogies

This section is designed to assist the reader in connecting the names of many individuals in the main body of the text to other families in the Potts Valley and Sweet Springs region (Alleghany, Craig, or Monroe Counties, under present boundaries.) The section does not attempt to include all families in the region-only those that pertain to this work. The research is drawn from various sources, particularly Louise Collins Perkins's extensive family studies and Nora Bragg Martin's family lineage studies. It updates the late Oren Morton's county histories in terms of current family lineage research.

Arritt Family. Michael Arritt (1773-1845) settled on Potts Creek in the first decade of the 1800s. He married first Mary Magdalene Wolf (1772-1832) and later Sarah Humphries. During the War of 1812, Michael hired Alexander Gray to serve in his stead in the 108th Virginia Militia. Michael served as justice and sheriff in Alleghany County.

Children of Michael and Mary: John Joseph (1796-1866), Jacob (1798-1799), Catherine (b. 1800), George W. (1802-1839), and Elizabeth (1805-1850). John Joseph married Elizabeth Bowyer (1807-ca. 1900).[1]

Baker Family. Jacob arrived with the Lewises at Sweet Springs and was employed as a baker at the resort. He adopted the occupational name as his surname. He married Christina Goliday (ca. 1761-1851).

Children of Jacob and Christina: Jacob (1788-1860).

Another family related to Jacob Baker-perhaps another son of Jacob-was that of David Madison Baker (d. 1840). David married Mary Bowyer, the daughter of Adam and Christina **Wolf** Bowyer.

Children of David and Mary: Jacob, Catherine, Madison, Anne, and Sarah.[2]

Bland Family. Robert Bland appeared in Greenbrier County about 1774. The spelling of name appears as "Blan" or "Blann" on some records. Robert, Sr. (d. 1795), had two military warrants and settled near Turkey Creek or Indian Creek in Monroe County next to Dunmore's War and Revolutionary War veteran Moses **Bostick**. Jesse Bland (d. 1835) was most likely Robert's brother.

Known children of Robert, Sr.: Joshua; Sally; Mary; Robert, Jr.; Alexander; Polly; Elizabeth; and Abigail.

Robert, Jr. (1784-1857) married Anna and moved near Peter's Mountain. They had at least three children: Esther E., James, and Joshua. Esther married James T. McKinney in 1813; James married India Dawson the same year; and Joshua married Polly Shires in 1807.

Alexander (d. 1857) married Sally Bostic, 1795. Children are listed under **Bostick**.

Joshua had at least one son, Robert, who married Elizabeth Hand in

1808.³

Booth Family. William, Sr., owned a tavern along the Sweet Springs-Fincastle stage route. He fell heavily into debt and sold the business in 1856 to David G. Givens.

Children: William, Jr.⁴

Bostic/Bostick Family. Moses (d. 1799) lived in the area by 1774, when he participated in Dunmore's War and the American Revolution. His wife Mary was alive in the early 1800s. The original family homestead appeared to near Turkey Creek or Dropping Lick, probably closer to the latter (near Crimson Springs, Monroe County, West Virginia) Alexander Bostick (1794-1869) settled near Willow Bend. It is uncertain how the two families are related, but they were at least cousins. Note Morton's remark about Moses and John as brothers; this is very unlikely. No original records were found linking the two as siblings, though some with father and son.

Children of Moses and Mary: John (ca. 1776-ca. 1835), Ruth, Eleanor, Margaret, Jonathan, Sarah, William, Thomas (ca. 1781-ca. 1855), Moses (ca. 1782-1862), and Mary (d. ca. 1825). John married Elizabeth **Bland** in 1795. Eleanor married Robert Fury in 1817. William married Ann Shaver. Mary was unmarried and moved to Ohio. Jonathan was blind.

Children of John and Elizabeth: Thomas, Archibald (1794-1869), Moses (d. ca. 1848), William (b. ca. 1803), John David (1806-1894),

Ruth, and Reuben (1811-1856). Reuben married Mary (Polly) Parker and died in a Monroe County smallpox epidemic in December 1856.

Children of Reuben: Martha (1835-1856), James A. (1839-1886), Mary E. (1843-1890), and Margaret (1847-ca. 1911). Reuben had a teacher, John Miles, living with them in the 1850 census. Martha died in the same smallpox epidemic that claimed her father. James married Jane **Jarvis** and served in the Confederate Army in Chapman's Battery. Mary E. married Dr. Samuel Chism (d. 1890) and had three children. Margaret married Confederate veteran Floyd Dodd in 1865.[5]

Callaghan Family. Dennis, an innkeeper of note, was an immigrant from Dublin, Ireland. His name was originally O'Callaghan. He married Margaret Atkinson in 1786. He settled in what was then Bath County in 1792 and soon operated his tavern and inn. He was still alive in 1813, but died a few years later.

Children of Dennis and Margaret: Oliver, William (b. 1793), Charles, Dennis, Boston, Thomas, Eleanor, Mary, and two Julias. One had previously died. It was an antebellum practice to reuse the name if desired. Oliver was an editor and politician in Alleghany County. William became a teacher.[6]

Cloyd Family. David (d. ca. 1790) was an immigrant to Virginia. His wife Margaret and son John were killed in an Indian massacre in 1745.

Children of David and Margaret: James (1731-ca. 1790), David (d. 1789), Michael (1735-1805), John (d. 1745), Elizabeth, Margaret,

Mary (1741-1827), and Joseph (d. 1742).

Elizabeth married James McDowell; Margaret married John Templeton. Governor James McDowell of Virginia is a descendant of this family. David married Elizabeth Woods and Joseph married Mary Gordon. Michael moved to Kentucky. Colonel Joseph moved to Montgomery County, Virginia, near the town of Dublin.

Children of Colonel Joseph and Mary Gordon: Gordon (1771-1833), Thomas (1774-1849), David (1776-1848), and Elizabeth.

Gordon became a general in the Virginia militia. He married his cousin Elizabeth McGavock.[7]

Dew Family. Samuel Dew, Sr. (1733-1810), of Richmond County on the Northern Neck of Virginia moved to Potts Creek in 1789, where he served as district court clerk. He married Betty (d. 1817).

Children of Samuel, Sr. and Betty: Sarah (b. ca. 1765), Charles (1767-1841), Mary, William, Samuel, Jr.(1771-1827), Elizabeth, Lucy (1775-1835), Peter, John (b. 1789). Of these children, Lucy, Elizabeth, and William stayed in the vicinity of Potts Creek. Lucy remained unmarried.[8]

Dunbar Family. Robert and his wife Hannah came to Gap Mills from Pennsylvania.

Children of Robert and Hannah: John M., Thomas (1795-1854),

Robert, William, Hannah, Elizabeth, Margaret, and Amanda.

William married Nancy **Jarvis**, Thomas married Mary Campbell. Both John M. and Robert married members of the Steele family. The Campbell and Steele families were both from the Gap Mills area.[9]

Ervine Family. Irishman Samuel Ervine (d. 1846) came to the Rich Patch Valley before 1810. He married Mary and had several children. Their son Joseph (1809-1892) was an active Presbyterian and a juror. He never married. Neither did his sisters Martha and Nancy. Two married sisters were Matilda Ervine Tinsley (d. 1849 in childbirth) and Sallie Ervine **Jarvis** (1811-1876). The one surviving child of Matilda, Franklin Tinsley, moved to Oregon.[10]

Fudge Family. Conrad (1771-1849), a native of Hanover, Germany, married a Persinger and lived around Blue Spring Run.

Children of Conrad: Alexander, Jacob, Andrew, Jonathan, Conrad R., Jeremiah, Maria L., Nancy, Catherine, Joseph, Stephen, Mary A., Elizabeth J., and Martha.

Andrew married Harriet K. Beale and served as county clerk from 1831 to 1858.[11]

Hook Family. Stephen owned an inn and tavern house in Rich Patch which was mentioned in the official records in December 1863. His son Madison (1811-1897) was a central political and entrepreneurial figure in the development of the Rich Patch turnpike. Madison married

Mary (1806-1865). Both are buried in the Hook family cemetery in the Rich Patch.

Children of Stephen: Madison, Henry, John, James, Elias, Beale (1832-1884), Sidney, and Caroline. Caroline married James Whitten. Their son William (1820-1849) is buried in the Hook family cemetery in Rich Patch.[12]

Jarvis family. Field Jarvis, Jr. (1756-1839), was born in Westmoreland County, Virginia. He arrived in the Potts Creek area about 1781 and settled in the region between Potts and Little Mountains. He married Asenith Adams in 1783.

Children of Field and Asenith: Mary Ann (1788-1859), Keziah (ca. 1783-1873), John Franklin (1791-1870), Field A. (1800-1890), Susannah (1786-1875), and Winnefred (1795-ca. 1850). Mary Ann (Polly) married William Neel. Susannah married John Barton **Linton**, who resided in the Potts Creek Valley near the old Sweet Springs stage road. John married Margaret **Dunbar** (1796-1878), and Nancy married William Dunbar (b. ca. 1792). Keziah married Obediah Pruitt and left for Gallia County, Ohio, in the 1820s. Subsequently Susannah went there as well. Field married Sally **Ervine** of the Rich Patch.

Children of John and Margaret: Hannah, Field Washington Jarvis (1824-1908), Asenith, Nancy (b. ca. 1829), and Mary S. (b. ca. 1840).

Hannah married Joseph Deeds in 1839. Field Washington, nicknamed

"Wash" Jarvis, was a Monroe County juror and official for many years. He married twice, the first time to Jane Steele of the Gap Mills area in 1845. Following her death, he married Diana Wakefield. Asenith married Chapman J. Cale in 1847.

Children of Field A. and Sally: Jane R. (1836-1927), Asenith M. (1835-1923), Mary Ann W. (1832-1923), John E. (1839-1907), Morgan T. (1847-1865), Joseph N. (1842-1927), and Virginia (1851-1921). Asenith and Mary A., called "Winnie" and "Matildie," respectively, were unmarried. Jane married James A. **Bostic** in 1861; John E. served as a Union soldier in the Civil War and lived in Ohio, Missouri, Texas, and Oklahoma. He married Mary Drake of Gallia County, Ohio in 1866. Joseph N. was also unmarried. Virginia married photographer John Wilson in Rich Patch and moved to Ronceverte, in Greenbrier County, West Virginia. Following Wilson's death, Virginia moved to Washington, DC.[13]

King Family. John and his wife Barbara were prosperous farmers in Rich Patch.

Children of John and Barbara: George, Charles, John, two daughters.

George was a successful tobacco producer and owned several curing barns. He also served in various official county capacities.[14]

Lewis Family. William (1724-1812) was the brother of the famous soldier Andrew Lewis. William settled in Sweet Springs about 1783. He married Ann Montgomery. He ran the springs as a fashionable resort and saw it from its infancy.

Children of William and Ann: John (1755-1823), Charles, Alexander, Thomas, Margaret, Agatha, and Elizabeth.

John achieved fame as a soldier in Dunmore's War and the American Revolution. He won the rank of major at the Battle of Monmouth in 1778. His wife was Mary Preston of Montgomery County, Virginia. Charles was a doctor.

Children of John and Mary: William Lynn, Margaret, Anne, Sarah, Polydora, John B., and Thomas.[15]

Linton Family. William Linton (ca. 1745-ca. 1815) was born in Prince William County, Virginia. He married Euphemia Nesbit (d. ca. 1830) and had four children: John Barton (d. ca. 1839), the eldest, James Nesbit (d. 1848), Elizabeth H., and Seth H. James was a veteran of the War of 1812 and married Rachel Humphreys. John married Susannah **Jarvis.**

Children of John and Susannah: Euphemia (b. ca. 1815), William (b. ca. 1817), Asenith A. (1818-1889), James Nesbit (1819-1904), Field J. (1820-1839), George A. (1824-1910), and Seth H. (ca. 1829-ca. 1864). Euphemia married John **Carson**; William married Rebecca **Dew**; and Asenith married Oliver Jones in 1836. James and Fielding remained unmarried. Seth married Nash **Persinger** of Alleghany County. Following the death of John B. Linton, his two youngest children, George and Seth, became wards of their uncle John F.

Jarvis. In the Civil War, Seth was killed attempting to see her husband in the Confederate Army, and Susannah, James, and Asenith left for Gallia County, Ohio. George made his adult home with his cousin Jane **Bostic** and her family.

Children of James and Rachel: William (d. 1911), Euphemia (d. 1911), Susan (d. 1907), and John B. (1844-1924).[16]

McAllister Family. Thompson (1811-1871) came from Adams County, Pennsylvania, in December 1849 and settled at an estate near Covington named Rose Dale. He entered the milling industry, and politically he became a Whig. He married Lydie Adams in 1839.

Children of Thompson and Lydie: Clara, Abraham Adams, William, E. Thompson, and Ann.[17]

Massie Family. Major Thomas Massie of New Kent County, Virginia, acquired land in the Falling Spring Valley near Rich Patch. He married Sarah Cocke in 1781. He lived primarily in Augusta County.

Children of Thomas and Sarah: Henry, Sr. (d. 1841).

Captain Henry Massie received the Falling Spring tract in 1814 after his marriage to Susan Preston Lewis of the Sweet Springs.

Children of Henry and Susan: Thomas, Sarah, Mary, Eugenia, Hezekiah, and Henry. Eugenia married a Gatewood.[18]

Pennell Family. Joseph (d. 1849) settled on Potts Creek and conducted his Methodist mission and many marriage ceremonies for many years. His wife was named Harriet.

Children of Joseph and Harriet: Lynch and Harriet.[19]

Persinger Family. This family was one of the earliest groups to settle on Potts Creek. Henry (ca. 1755-1824) and his brother Jacob settled on Blue Spring Run. Henry married Griselda.

Known children of Henry and Griselda: Mary (b. 1775), John (b. ca. 1777), Andrew (b. ca. 1779), Jacob (b. ca. 1780), Margaret (b. ca. 1793), Sally (b. ca. 1795), Elizabeth (b. ca. 1796), Rebecca (b. ca. 1797), Sampson (b. ca. 1798), and Ruth (b. ca. 1805). Andrew lived along Potts Creek near the Rich Patch and married Martha.

Children of Andrew: Aaron, Zebidee, Nash, John, Martha, Mary, Martin, and Adeline. Nash served in the Civil War as a private in the Confederate forces. Aaron and Zebedee were briefly imprisoned during the conflict.[20]

Rose Family. Alexander was said to have come from King George County, Virginia, to Botetourt County about 1770.

Children of Alexander: Obediah (ca. 1765-1827), Joseph, Rebecca, and Jane.

Obediah and Joseph surveyed lands for the Cloyd family along Sinking

Creek in the early 1790s. Obediah never married, but Joseph married Catherine Bousman in 1790.

Children of Joseph and Catherine: Joseph Henry (1793-1850), Elizabeth (b. ca. 1794), James (1796-1840), and Charles C. (ca. 1798-1881).

Joseph H. was said to have been married several times, once to Susan Daugherty in March 1815 and perhaps earlier to Kurene (Karenhappock or Agnes) Terry in December 1813.

Known children of Joseph H.: William W. (d. 1895), Jackson (ca. 1815-1862)

William Washington Rose was a sheriff in Alleghany County. Jackson married Ruth Wolf in 1837 and died in the Civil War.[21]

Skeen Family. William Skeen (1818-1893) was a local politician and lawyer in Covington. Robert attended the August 1844 and November 1846 internal improvement conventions at Lewisburg and Covington, respectively. William was present at the Covington Convention.[22]

Stull Family. Daniel settled in the Rich Patch. His son James married Hannah King. Another son, Jacob, married Phoebe Bennett. Daniel's daughter Mary married Jacob Bennett.[23]

Taylor Family. Hugh Paul Taylor (d. 1831) was born near Lexington and lived for a time in Lewisburg before settling in Covington and working as an attorney. He served as a state engineer and militia soldier as well. As claimed by Oren T. Morton, Taylor wrote much of what became *Chronicles of Border Warfare*. He also wrote much on internal improvements and the Native American history of the area. Taylor died before many of the improvements issues were dealt with. His wife was Mary Ann Woltz. He had a sister, Betsy Taylor Steele, and a brother, Stuart Taylor.

Children of Hugh: Alexander, Henry, and Virginia.[24]

Walker Family. Andrew Walker and his Elizabeth came to the Potts Creek area about 1780.

Children of Andrew and Elizabeth: Henry and John.

Henry and John were both postal contractors who owned stagecoaches. Eventually they ran the Mountain House, a tavern house on the Sweet Springs-Fincastle stage road. Henry became a militia captain and married Maria Shawver, daughter of the owner of the Shawver Tavern. John was a bachelor and ran the Mountain House until it burned down in 1860. The fire was said to have been started by a spurned lover.

Children of Henry and Maria: Margaret, Sophia, Sallie, Mary, Julia, Maria, Emma, and Wade.

Margaret married James Rogers, an investor in the Sweet Springs-Fincastle Stage road improvement.[25]

Wright Family. Peter (d. 1793) was a tavernkeep by 1780. Peter's Mountain is said to have been named for him; legend has it that he slept in a cave in a blanketing snowdrift. He married Jane (d. 1807).

Children of Peter and Jane: Rachel, Elizabeth, Agnes, Jane, Martha, Sarah, Mary, Thomas, James, William, Peter, and Rebecca.

Thomas was a captain in the Revolution. Several of this generation moved to Kentucky and beyond.[26]

Appendix A.-Virginia Militia
108th Regiment-War of 1812

Explanatory Note: Arrangement is the same as in the original document. From RG15, National Archives.

A List of Fines instituted by the Court of Enquiry held for the 108<u>th</u> Reg.t in the year 1814 and put into the hands of the Sheriff of Monroe County in the year 1815 for collection to wit

Ashley Richard $	.75
Aldridge Wm	.75
Alexander Matthew	1.50
Arnot Jesse	.75
Abbott John	.75

	4.50
Baggwell Nickolas	.75
Beirne George	.75
Bush James	1.50
B [unreadable] William	1.50
Bowyer Thomas	2.25
Burns George	1.50
Broyles Daniel	.75
Bland James	.75
Bayles Hugh	.75
Broyles Solomon	.75
Bland Robert	3.00
Baker David	2.25
Bland Wm	.75
Bryson James	.75
Brown William	.75
Burdit Giles jr	.75
Burdit Joseph	1.50
Burdit Miles	.75
	$21.15

Crooks, Robert	.75
Cummins Hugh	.75
Campbell Andw	.75
Cummins Absolem	.75
Crider Peter	.75
Carter Jonathan	1.50
Condonell James	.75
Cart George	.75
Callaway Andrew	.75
Crawford Zachariah	.75
Canterberry Erskine	1.50
Cloud Nathaniel	.75
Carper Isaac	3.00
Clark William	.75
Cornwell William	.75
Callaway Joshua	.75
	$15.85
Drum Jacob	.75
Damron John	.50
Dolin John	.75
Daugherty William	.75
	3.75
Earley John	.75
Evans William	.75
Edes Catton	.75
Engleton William	1.50
Estill John	.75
Ellison Francis	.75
	5.25
Ferrell Christopher	1.50
Fink Casper	1.50
Fife Edward	.75
Fudge David	.75

same	.75
Felding Adam	1.50
Floro(?) James	.75
James Fadey	.75
Farley Gideon	.75
	9.00
Gulkett William	.75
Gregory Samuel	.75
Gray Alexander	.75
Gray Robert	1.50
	3.75
Hayes F. Isaac	.75
Harmon Peter	1.50
same	.75
Hoke William	.75
Hickenbottom James	.75
Joseph Haynes Jr	.75
John Haynes	.75
	5.00
Hollseign William	
Jones Joseph	.75
Insco Jesse	.75
	1.50
Kelly Robert	.75
Kilburn Amos	.75
	1.50
Leach Joshua	.75
Linton B. John	.75
Lynch William	.75

Lynch Samuel	.75
Larreme James	.75
Lowe John	.75
Lowry Thomas	.75
	5.25
Lewis Charles	1.00
	6.25
Maggert David	.75
Maggert Joseph	1.50
Mogaret David	.75
McCallister James	1.50
Maddy William	.75
Moss Henry	.75
McMahan William	1.50
Morgin Jesse	.75
Moore James	.75
Moss Mathew	.75
M Colgin John	.75
	10.50
Neel Hugh	.75
Nelson William	.75
Nettle John	.75
	2.25
Powel William	.75
Phillips Alix	1.50
	XXXXXX
Powel Shelton	.75
Perry Robert	.75
Penington Wheeler	.75
Pine Squire	.75

Pine William	.75
Phips John	3.75
Peck Jacob	1.50
Peters Christian	.75
	12.00

Rains Samuel	.75
Rose H. Joseph	1.50
Roales Mordakiah	1.50
James Rose	1.50
John Rains	1.50
Raines Wm	.75
	7.50

Sprouse James	.75
Smith Wm	.75
Simmons Joab	1.50
Spar John J	1.50
Scott Thomas	.75
Stone John	.75
Sey(?) Abraham	.75
Stickler John	1.50
Sticker Daniel	.75
Seiers James	.75
Shewmate Tolison	.75
Spangler Charles	.75
Swinney James jr	.75
	12.00

Thompson John	1.50
Thompson James	3.75
Tomison John	.75
Thompson Samuel	.75
Thompson William	.75
Thompson Charles	.75

	8.25
Vass John	.75
Wylie Thomas	.75
Wolf Abraham	1.50
Wolf John	1.50
Woinstaff Jacob	.75
Jacob Wolf	.75
Weir John	1.50
Windleblack John	1.50
Walker William	1.50
Willis Amile	.75
Woodram Richard	.75
Woodville James	2.25
Young David	.75
Zoll William	2.25
	17.25

1815 May 9th
Then recd of Isaac Hutchison Clerk of 108th Regt of militia. Ticketts for fines imposed by said regt aginable to the foregoing list which I will collect or acct for with the commonwealth of Virginia as the law directs

        M Erskine CS for

Appendix B.

Explanatory Note: The following is a partial roster of Company K, U.S. Volunteers (or Voltiguers), for the Mexican War. It was found among papers in the Thornton T. Perry Manuscripts, Virginia Historical Society (Mss1P4299g32). The enlistees below numbered 15 to 45 are missing. Transcription is as true as possible to the original; so spelling may not be accurate.

Mexican War 1847
Company-K US Volunteers

Captn James H Calwell

1st Lieut Jno Wickham Leigh
2nd Lieut George W Carr
Brevt 2d Lieut-J W Smith

Enlisted at
White Sulphur Springs,
Greenbrier County Va

Seageants
Coleman
Wilson

Corporals

Craft
Caldwell

Privates	where Enlisted
1 Adams S.B.	Fincastle
2 Baker Hurum	White Sulp
3 Ball Reuben	Monroe
4 Beard James L	Charleston
5 Burns John M	Union
6 Bunxs	
7 Caldwell Madison A	White Sul
8 Catterton D.C.	Albemarle
9 Clark	

10	Coleman R.S	Albemarle
11	Craft Geo. W	Covington
12	Craig David C	Gauley Bridge
13	Crawford William J	Albemarle
14	Cunningham Jacob	White Sul

[skips to 46-2nd page]

46	Parrish Joseph	Albemarle
47	Pawpaw John	Fincastle
48	Ramsay (1) Wm A.	Gauley Bridge
49	Ramsey (2)	
50	Roboy William	Albemarle
51	Rucker Ballard	White Sulp
52	Shouse	
53	Smith John A	Rockbridge
54	Starkes Cary P	White Sul
55	Stover William	Charlottesville
56	Tanner Lewis H	Gauley
57	Taylor Alexander M.	White Sul
58	Thompson Larkin	Monroe
59	Waid John	Anthy Creek [Anthony]
60	Wilcher Thos H	Fincastle
61	Williams (1) John	Albemarle
62	Williams (2) Peter	Blue Sul
63	Williams (3)	
64	Wilkerson Nelson	Albemarle
65	Wantz_Robert	Lewisburg
66	Kirby	Albemarle
67	Bass Robert	ditto
68	Wm H Sly	White Sulphur
69	Roberts Richard	ditto

Lieut Carr 4 men names not reported
"   Leigh 2   <u>ditto</u>

6-

Notes
Chapter 1

1. Frances Logan, *The Old Sweet: Biography of a Spring* (Roanoke, VA: n.p., 1940), 13.

2. Bessie Rowland James, *Ann Royall's USA* (New Brunswick, NJ: Rutgers University Press, 1972), 26; Oren Morton, *A Centennial History of Alleghany County* (repr., Harrisonburg, Va: C.J. Carrier Company, 1986), 97-98.

3. James, *Ann Royall's USA*, 29; Ibid., 51; Morton, *Centennial History*, 98; Deed in Roane v. Royall, Case File Box 235, Circuit Court, Staunton, VA; James, *Ann Royall's USA*, 31-33.

4. Affidavits of James N. Linton, Christopher Shawver, Jacob Shawver in Roane v. Royall, Case File Box 235; James, *Ann Royall's USA*, 51; Marcellus Zimmerman, "The Zimmerman Papers-Sketches of Dr. McElhenney's Scholars by Marcellus Zimmerman,"*Journal of the Greenbrier Historical Society*, 3, 2 (1976), 92-93.

5. James, *Ann Royall's USA*, 39; Ibid., 10; Ibid., 28; Ibid., 67-69; Morton, *Alleghany County*, 99; James, *Ann Royall's USA*, 71-72.

6. James, *Ann Royall's USA*, 55; Ibid., 68-69; Oren T. Morton, *A History of Monroe County, West Virginia (*Baltimore, MD: Regional Publishing Company, 1980), 370; Morton, *Alleghany*, 98-100.

7. Historical Booklet: *Greenbrier County 160th Anniversary 1778-1938* (Charleston, WV: Jarrett Printing Company, 1938), 2-3.

8. Morton, *History of Monroe*, 370-71.

9. "Genealogy of the Lewis Family," *West Virginia Historical Magazine Quarterly*, 4, 2 (1904), 145-46; Morton, *Monroe*, 201-3.

10. Morton, *Monroe*, 370.

11. James McHenry to wife Peggy, September 16, 1794, in Bernard C. Steiner, ed., *The Papers of James McHenry* (New York, NY: Arno Press, 1979), 120-121.

12. Gay Arritt, "Dr. James Merry Was Founder of Covington," *Covington Virginian*, 9 October 1964; Harry W. Walton, Jr., "Covington's Name was Mouth of Dunlap," *Covington Virginian*, 15 March 1986; Alleghany County Schools, unpublished paper, *Early History of Alleghany County*, 4.

13. Governor's Message, *Journal of the House of Delegates, 1826*, 5. Cited in Paul Douglas Linkenhoker, *A History of Schooling in Alleghany County, Clifton Forge, and Covington, Virginia* (Ann Arbor, MI: University Microfilms, 1993), doctoral dissertation, Virginia Polytechnic Institute, 12-13.

14. *A Synopsis of the James River and Kanawha Improvement, with a View to the Value and Productiveness of the Capital Stock of the Company* (n.p., 1833), 3; Wayland Fuller Dunaway, *History of the James River and Kanawha Company* (New York, NY: AMS Press, 1969), from HISTORY OF THE JAMES RIVER AND KANAWHA COMPANY by Wayland Fuller Dunway. Copyright © 1922 by Columbia University Press. Reprinted with permission of the publisher, 52.

15. *Early History of Alleghany County*, 4; Morton, *Alleghany*, 43.

16. "Dennis Callaghan," *West Virginia Historical Magazine Quarterly*, 4, 4 (October 1904), 328-29; James, *Ann Royall's USA*, 28; Ibid., 97; Marshall de Bruhl, *Sword of San Jacinto: A Life of Sam Houston* (New York, NY: Random House, 1993), 21; James, *Ann Royall's USA*, 28; Ibid., 97; "Historic Sites on the Stage Road," Works Progress Administration, Historical Inventory, Alleghany County, Virginia State Library; "Stringer Tavern," WPA, Historical Inventory, Alleghany County, Virginia State Library.

17. Morton, *Alleghany*, 71.

18. Robert Douthat Stoner, *A Seed Bed of the Republic: A Study of the Pioneers in the Upper (Southern) Valley of Virginia* (Kingsport, TN: Kingsport Press, 1962), 255; Morton, *Alleghany*, 43.

19. Sons of Temperance, Chapter No. 244, Journal, Duke University Special Collections.

20. Dwight Wickline, "The Circuit Riders," *The Monroe Watchman*, April 27, 1995.

21. RG 15, Muster Rolls, August 31 and October 31, 1814, Box 271, National Archives; John M. Hallahan, *The Battle of Craney Island: A Matter of Credit* (Portsmouth, VA: Saint Michael's Press, 1986), 41.

Chapter 2

1. Morton, *Monroe*, 201-3; Stan Cohen, *Historic Springs of the Virginias* (Charleston, WV: Pictorial Histories Publishing Company, c.1981), 164; Logan, *The Old Sweet*, 14-15.

2. Morton, *Monroe*, 203-04.

3. James McHenry to wife Peggy, September 7, 1789, in Bernard C. Steiner, *James McHenry*, 120-121.

4. Ibid., 121.

5. McHenry to wife Peggy, August 8, 1794, in Steiner, *James McHenry*, 146.

6. McHenry to wife Peggy, August 24, 1794, in Steiner, *James McHenry*, 149.

7. Morton, *Monroe*, 232; Ibid., opposite 232.

8. McHenry to wife Peggy, September 16, 1794, in Steiner, *James McHenry*, 152.

9. McHenry to wife Peggy, September 28, 1794, in Steiner, *James McHenry*, 153.

10. Dabney Minor to John Brown, Jr., October 10, 1799, in Logan, *The Old Sweet*, 3-4.

11. Minor to Brown, Jr., October 10, 1799, in Logan, *The Old Sweet*, 4.

12. John Howell Briggs, "Journal of a Trip to the Sweet Springs, Commencing July 23d and ending September 29th 1804," in Virginia Historical Society, *First Resorts: A Visit to Virginia's Springs* (Richmond, VA: n.p., 1987), 5-6.

13. Logan, *The Old Sweet*, 35; Frederick T. Newbraugh, ed. *The Life and Adventures of Robert Bailey: An Autobiography-Originally Published Richmond, VA 1822.* (Berkeley Spring, WV: Warm Springs Echoes Book Company, 1978), title page; Stoner, *Seed Bed*, 172-73.

14. Briggs, "Journal," in Virginia Historical Society, *First Resorts*, 22.

15. Will Price, "Doctor Sings Praises of Red Sweet Springs, *Alleghany Highlander*, 20 October, 1982.

16. John J. Moorman, "The Memoir of Dr. John J. Moorman: Resident Physician at White Sulphur Springs," *Journal of the Greenbrier Historical Society*, 3, 6 (1980), 8.

17. Ibid.

18. Peggy Dow, *The Life, Travels, Labors, and Writings of Lorenzo Dow; Including his Singular and Erratic Wanderings in Europe and America. To which is added His Chain Journey from Babylon to Jerusalem; Dialogue Between Curious and Singular; Hints on the Fulfillment of Prophecy, Etc., Etc. and the Vicissitudes, or Journey of Life, and Supplementary Reflections by Peggy Dow* (New

York, NY: United States Book Company, 1836), 338-39; Ibid., Lorenzo Dow, *History of Cosmopolite: Or the Four Volumes of Lorenzo's Journal Concentrated into One: Containing his Experience & Travels, from Childhood to 1814, being Upwards of Thirty-Six Years* (New York, NY: John C. Totten, 1814), 465-66.

19. Logan, *The Old Sweet*, 11; Ibid., 15; John Lewis Inventory, 1823, Alleghany County Wills and Inventories Book 1, 22-23, Alleghany County Courthouse.

20. Cohen, *Historic Springs of the Virginias*, 164; Logan, *The Old Sweet*, 5; Agnes E. Gish, "The Rat Room of Monroe County's Court House Reveals Secret to the Old Sweet Springs Past," *Monroe Watchman*, 20 October, 1994. Thanks to Dr. Ronald Ripley for his insights on the Sweet Springs design.

21. Perceval Reniers, *The Springs of Virginia: Life, Love, and Death at the Waters 1775-1900* from THE SPRINGS OF VIRGINIA by Perceval Renier. Copyright © 1941 by the University of North Carolina Press. Used by permission of the publisher, 150-52.

22. Cohen, *Historic Springs of the Virginias*, 164; Logan, *The Old Sweet*, 4-5; Quintard Taylor, *White Sulphur Springs: A Brief History* (n.p., 1923), 41.

23. Reniers, *The Springs of Virginia*, 28-30.

24. Cohen, *Historic Springs of the Virginias*, 158; Morton, *Monroe*, 208; Reniers, *Springs of Virginia*, 45.

25. Louise Rawl, *Traveling Heritage Road* (Ronceverte, WV: Fairlea Printers and Publishers, 1969), 2; Taylor, *White Sulphur Springs*, 19; Ibid., 39.

26. Ibid.

27. Cohen, *Historic Springs of the Virginias*, 119.

28. Morton, *Monroe*, 206; Reniers, *Springs of Virginia*, 176-178.

29. James, *Anne Royall's USA*, 55-57; Ibid., 62-3; Ibid., 395-96n1.

30. Elizabeth Shawver testimony, July 15, 1815, Roane v. Royall.

31. Jacob Shawver testimony, July 15, 1814, Roane v. Royall; James, *Ann Royall's USA*, 63; James Linton testimony, July 15, 1814, Roane v. Royall.

32. James, *Ann Royall's USA*, 57; Ibid., 61-63; Morton, *Alleghany*, 99; James, *Ann Royall's USA*, 81-82.

33. Exhibit A No. 9, Deed of 480 Acres at the Sweet Springs, Roane v. Royall; James, *Ann Royall's USA*, 35-36; Ibid., 27-28; John Lewis Deposition, July 15, 1814.

34. James, *Ann Royall's USA*, 67; Elizabeth Carson testimony, August 1, 1814, Roane v. Royall.

35. Morton, *Alleghany*, 99; Ibid.; 102.

36. Zimmerman, "Sketches," 92-93; James, *Ann Royall's USA*, 51; Ibid., 83; Ibid., 88.

37. John Lewis Will, Lewis Inventory, 1823, Alleghany County Wills and Inventories No. 1, 22-23, Alleghany County Courthouse.

38. "Genealogy of the Lewis Family," *West Virginia Historical Magazine Quarterly*, 4, 2 (1904), 146; Morton, *Monroe*, 370-71; Ibid., 419; *Dedication of the Governor John Floyd Memorial Monument-Sunday, August 23, 1964-3:00 P.M., EDST-Sweet Springs, West Virginia*, program; Horton P. Beirne, ed., *Historical Sketches by Gay Arritt* (Covington, VA: Alleghany Historical Society, 1982), 88.

39. Morton, *Monroe*, 370-71; Ibid., 206.

40. Zimmerman, "Sketches," 30; Morton, *Monroe*, 206; Ibid., 203; Ibid., 27.

41. James, *Ann Royall's USA*, 66; James N. Linton Settlement Papers, loose, Monroe Courthouse, Union, WV; Morton, *Monroe*, 322.

42. Depositions taken at Sweet Springs, June 30, 1843, William Booth, Sr. v. John B. Linton's Admr, Alleghany County Courthouse, Covington, VA.

43. Decree, May 11, 1847, F.A. Jarvice v Jno Dodd, Case 105, Loose Papers, Union, WV.

44. Ibid.; Morton, *Monroe*, 360; Ibid., 466.

45. Monroe, *Monroe*, 192; Ibid., 206.

46. Ibid.; J. J. Moorman, *A Guide to the Virginia Springs: giving, in addition to the Routes and Distances, Description of the Springs, and also of The Natural Curiosities of the State.* (Staunton, VA: Robert Cowan, 1851), title page; Ibid., xi-xii.

47. Ibid., 34.

48. Logan, *The Old Sweet*, 30-31; R. Lewis Wright, *Artists in Virginia Before 1900: An Annotated Checklist* (Charlottesville, VA: University Press of Virginia, 1983), 9-10.

49. Dorothy Gilchrist, *The Virginia Springs: A Mirror of Ante-Bellum Society*(1943) M.A. Thesis, University of Virginia, 108-09.

Chapter 3

1."Old Inn Served As Haven Back In Stage Coach Era," *Roanoke Times*, 2 October, 1938.

2. "Booth-Givens Tavern," Works Progress Administration, Historical Inventory, Alleghany County, Virginia State Library.

3. Ibid.

4. Memorial, December 27, 1827, Alleghany County Legislative Petitions 1823-39, A15, A646, 8911, Virginia State Archives.

5. Ibid. The other signitures on the memorial were: Alexander Sawyer, Henry Humphreys, Alex H. Terrill, Isaac Wolf, Diocletian Reynolds, Hamilton Bess, R. Mannspike, Charles Fridley, Isaac Fridley, Sampson Wolf, Henry Humphries, Sampson Persinger, James Davison, Joseph Pern, William Humphries, Jacob Bennet, William Johnston, Peter Booth, Adam Maggar, George Aritt, Bernard Johnston, James Gilleland, David and John Bowyer, James Johnston, Jacob Wolf, John Rinehart, Moses Anders, George W. And Abraham Wolf, William Terry, Frederick, George, John and Abraham Armentrout, Daniel Alford, Alexander Kitchen, Alexander Rayhill, Oliver Callaghan, Hugh Paul Taylor, Denison Rose, Archibald Kincaid, William Kyle, John Aritt, Richard Smith, George Lemmon, Alex Johnson, Nathan Bush, John Callaghan, John Holloway, M. Pitzer, G. Harman, James [illegible], Peter Helmintoller, John B. Linton, Andrew Nickell, John Shawver, William Harman, Charles Dew, James Oiler, John Wolf Jr., William A. Mastin, Andrew Wilson, Jacob Armentrout, Anthony Bronomer, Abraham Wolf Jr., James Kimberlin, Alexander Fleet, Conrad Fudge, Andrew Kincaid, and Jacob Huffman. All of these individuals (with the exception of a few, such as the Callaghans) were from the Potts Creek area or Covington.

6. Ibid.; Morton, *Alleghany*, 43; C.C. Pearson and J. Edwin Hendricks, *Liquor and Anti-Liquor in Virginia, 1619-1919* (Durham, NC: Duke University Press, Copyright 1967), 73. Reprinted with permission; Ibid., 97; Ibid., 13.

7. Sons of Temperance, *Journal*, title page.

8. Ellen Eslinger, "Antebellum Liquor Reform in Lexington, Virginia: The Story of a Small Southern Town," *Virginia Magazine of History and Biography*, 99 (April 1991), 168; Ibid., 170.

9. Otis K. Rice, *History of Greenbrier County* (Parsons, WV: McClain, 1986) 211-13.

10. Ibid., 213; Monroe County Historical Society, *A Sprightly Village: A Walking Tour of Historic Union, W.V.* (Union, WV: Monroe County Historical Society, n.d.), no. 30, brochure.

11. Pearson and Hendricks, *Liquor and Anti-Liquor*, 73; Ibid., 97; Sons of Temperance, *Journal*.

12. Sons of Temperance, *Journal*; Morton, *Alleghany*, 154; Ibid., 149-150.

13. Alleghany County Petitions 1840-62, February 12, 1853, A704, 18610, Virginia State Archives.

14. Sons of Temperance, *Journal*.

15. Ibid.

16. Ibid.

17. *Minutes of the Grand Division of the Sons of Temperance, of the State of Virginia, At an Adjourned Session, held in Richmond, June 1, 1852; and of the Regular Quarterly Session, Held in the Town of Fincastle July 28, 1852.* (Richmond, VA: H.K. Ellyson, 1852), Title Page; Ibid., 329.

18. Pearson and Hendricks, *Liquor and Anti-Liquor*, 150; Ibid., 150n.

19. Rice, *Greenbrier*, 228-29.

20. Charles Henry Ambler, *Thomas Ritchie: a Study in Virginia*

Politics (Richmond, VA: Bell Book & Stationary Company, 1913), 149.

21. Rice, *Greenbrier*, 224; Ibid., 230; Ibid., 245; Ambler, *Sectionalism in Virginia*, 222-23; Ibid., 227.

22. *Lewisburg Alleghanian*, 6 September, 1833 from Rice, *Greenbrier*, 232; John Goode Testimony, Question 40, September 9, 1872, Southern Claims Commission, Claim 14704, National Archives.

23. Rice, *Greenbrier*, 230-31; Ibid., 233-34; "Republican Whig Ticket," 1836 Broadside, Lewis Family Papers, University of Virginia.

24. *Biographical Directory of the United States Congress 1774-1989-The Continental Congress September 5, 1774 to October 21, 1788 and the Congress of the United States From the First Through the One-Hundredth Congress March 4, 1789 to January 3, 1989, Inclusive* (Washington, DC: Government Printing Office, 1989), 741.

25. Zimmerman, "Sketches," 26-27; Bernard Mayo, ed., "Henry Clay, Patron and Idol of White Sulphur Springs: His Letters to James Calwell," *Virginia Magazine of History and Biography*, 55 (October 1947), 301-03; Ibid., 304-05.

26. Moorman, "Memoir," 13.

27. Clay to Calwell, June 30, 1832, in Mayo, "Henry Clay, Patron," 307.

28. "When Henry Clay Came to Union," miscellaneous clipping. Found in the Virginia Historical Society's file of the Caperton Papers, this clipping was most likely from the *Monroe Watchman*, probably dated about 1890, since it mentioned "older citizens" still remembering Clay; Laura E. Armitage, 1835 entry, *James River & Kanawha Co.: extracts from Minutes 1835-1840 Regarding of Location of Canal and Condemned Properties-Extracts from Minutes-1865-Reopening of Canal After War Between the States*, typescript, Virginia State Archives.

29. Clay to Peyton, May 11, 1841, reprinted from Robert Seager II and Melba Porter Hay, ed., *The Papers of Henry Clay: The Whig Leader-January 1, 1837-December 31, 1843, Vol. 9*, copyright © 1988 by The University Press of Kentucky, by permission, 533.

30. "To the Republican Voters of Botetourt," 1840 broadside, University of Virginia.

31. Stoner, *Seed Bed*, 224.

32. "Whig State Convention," 1840 broadside, University of Virginia; Governor's Poll, December 8, 1851, Loose Papers, Union, WV.

33. Ibid.

34. RG29, M33, *Population Schedules of the Fourth Census of the United States*, Monroe County, 39th Division, 463; Craig County Order Book 2, 1860-63; Orville Bostic interview, Annandale, VA, April 1988; Governor's Poll.

35. Layman Reynolds interview, Keenan, WV, September 1991; Morton, *Monroe*, 335-36; Governor's Poll.

36. Ibid.

37. Ibid.; Morton, *Monroe*, 335-36; Ibid., 384; Ibid., 390; Orville Bostic Interview, Annandale, VA, April 1988; Morton, *Monroe*, 330.

38. Governor's Poll.

39. Ibid.; RG 15, Revolutionary War Pension and Bounty-Land Warrant Application Files-Field Jarvis, M804, Roll 1408; Orville Bostic Interview, Annandale, VA, April 1988; Notes on Bostic Cemetery, Paint Bank, Virginia; Morton, *Monroe*, 384; WPA, *Monroe County, West Virginia, Volume 3, Wills and Inventory* (Washington, DC: typed and in possession of the Daughters of the American

Revolution, 1936), 16; Ibid., 41; Morton, *Monroe*, 384; William Booth, Sr. v. J.B. Linton's Admr., Alleghany County Courthouse.

40. Governor's Poll.

41. Bernard Caperton, *The Caperton Family* (Charlottesville, VA: n.p., 1973), 69; Ibid., 77; John Frederick Dorman, *The Prestons of Smithfield and Greenfield in Virginia: descendants of John and Elizabeth (Patton) Preston Through Five Generations* (Louisville, KY: Filson Club, 1982), 260-61; Ibid., 266-67.

42. Kenneth W. Noe, *Southwest Virginia's Railroad: Modernization and the Sectional Crisis* (Chicago, IL: University of Illinois Press, 1994), 88.

43. Ambler, *Thomas Ritchie*, 244-45; Ibid., 231. Note that Angus McDonald was a political figure in western Virginia who resided near Romney.

44. Noe, *Southwest Virginia's Railroad*, 88-89; Howard P. Nash, Jr., *Third Parties in American Politics* (Washington, DC: Public Affairs Press, 1959), 7.

45. Noe, *Southwest Virginia's Railroad*, 88-89; Nash, *Third Parties*, 7; Ibid., 15; Ibid., 21.

46. Morton, *Monroe*, 134; Monroe County Petitions 1840-50, December 31, 1846, B3503, 15235, Virginia State Archives; Ibid., Monroe County Petitions, December 29, 1849, B3511, 16846; Monroe County Petitions, January 22, 1850.

47. Monroe County Petitions 1840-50, December 17, 1850; Morton, *Monroe*, 134; Ibid., December 8, 1841, B3496, 13096, Virginia State Archives.

48. *Dedication of the Alleghany County, Virginia-Monroe County, West Virginia Boundary Monument-Sunday, August 23, 1964-3:00 P.M., DST-Sweet Springs, West Virginia* program. Found in the

purchased papers of Reo Baker, Sweet Springs, VA.

49. Alleghany County Legislative Petitions, February 9, 1852, Virginia State Archives.

50. "Petition of Many Citizens of Alleghany Cty. Praying that a Precinct Election may be Established at the House of Jno. Mastin in said Cty," February 24, 1840, Alleghany County Legislative Petitions 1840-62, B16, A694, 12943, Virginia State Archives.

51. Ibid.

52. Ibid.; Gertrude Lacy, *A Walking Tour of Old Covington-Historic & Architectural* (n.p., 1981), 13.

53. Morton, *Alleghany*, 44.

54. Ibid.; F. Johnson, *Memorials of Old Virginia Clerks, Arranged Alphabetically by Counties with Complete Index of Names and Dates of Service From 1634 to the Present Time* (Lynchburg, VA: J.P. Bell Company, 1888), 34-36.

55. *Fincastle Mirror*, August 22, 1823, Virginia State Archives.

56. *Fincastle Mirror*, July 23, 1824, Virginia State Archives.

57. Morton, *Alleghany*, 150-51; Morton, *Morton*, 466.

58. O. Callaghan to William Callaghan, 25th, July, 1833, in Harold H. Haines, *The Callaghan Mail 1821-1859: A Book Featuring the Lives of William Callaghan, Missouri Pioneer and his Slave Isaac Crawford: Indians, Big Game, Gold and Old Letters* (Hannibal, MO: author, 1949), 32-33.

59. O. Callaghan to William Callaghan, 28th, June, 1834, in Haines, *The Callaghan Mail*, 33. Steele was Callaghan's estranged brother-in-law.

60. Ibid.

61. Johnson, *Memorials of Old Virginia Clerks*, 166.

62. Morton, *Monroe*, 464-67; Morton, *Alleghany*, 153.

63. Morton, *Alleghany*, 149; "Fincastle Internal Improvements Convention." in *Fincastle Democrat*, November 1845, Virginia State Archives. Filed with January 9, 1846 Legislative Petitions, Alleghany County, 1840-62; Morton, *Monroe*, 464; Ibid., 325.

Chapter 4

1. Morton, *Monroe*, 211-12.

2. Linkenhoker, *History of Schooling*, 11; Henry Ruffner, "Dennis Calaghan." in the *West Virginia Historical Magazine Quarterly*, 4 (April 1904), 328-29; Taylor, *White Sulphur Springs*, 29.

3. Alex L. ter Braake, "Postal History of the James River and Kanwaha Turnpike," from the Annual of the American Philatelic Congress (1970). Reprinted in *West Virginia History*, 33 (October 1971), 36; Ibid., 40.

4. William Couper, *Claudius Crozet: Soldier-Scholar-Educator-Engineer (1789-1864)* (Charlottesville, VA: Historical Publishing Company, 1936), 33n; Ibid., 33-34.

5. Morton, *Alleghany*, 59.

6. Rice, *Greenbrier*, 231.

7. Hugh Paul Taylor, Application for Employment as Assistant Engineer, March 24, 1829, Box 49, Board of Public Works, Virginia State Archives, Richmond.

8. Ibid.; John Wood or Herman Boye Map of Virginia, original plat from Alleghany Court House, Covington, VA, 1821;

9. Reprinted by permission Louisiana State University Press from *Thomas Mann Randolph, Jefferson's Son-in-Law*, by William H. Gaines, Jr. Copyright © 1966 by Louisiana State University Press, 119.

10. Alleghany County Petition for the extension of the Baltimore & Ohio Rail Road, December 10, 1827, Alleghany County Legislative Petitions, 1823-39, A15, A647, 8912, Virginia State Archives, Richmond; Dunaway, *History of the James River*, 80.

11. Alleghany County Petition, December 10, 1827, Virginia State Archives.

12. *Speech of George W. Summers, of Kanawha, Before the State Convention of Virginia, in the Committee of the Whole, on the Basis of Representation March 18, 1851* (Richmond, VA: William Culley, n.d.), 39.

13. Couper, *Crozet*, 48; Ibid., 55-56; Dunaway, *History of the James River*, 75-76; Ibid., 83.

14. Virginia State Library, "Turnpike Companies," in Earl G. Swem, *Bulletin Virginia State Library: A Bibliography of Virginia* (Richmond, VA: Davis Bottom, Superintendent Public Printing, 1916), 1026; Ibid., 1028-1029; Ibid., 1030-1031.

15. *Journal and Proceedings of the Lewisburg Convention Convened on the 31st of October, 1831, To Deliberate on the Subject of Internal Improvement in Virginia* (Kanawha C.H., VA: Campbell & Walker, 1831), 15; "Memorial of the Covington Convention," Document No. 20, in *Journal of the House of Delegates of the State of Virginia* (Richmond, VA: Samuel Shepherd, 1846), 1-2; *A Synopsis of the James River and Kanawha Improvement, with a View to the Value and Productiveness of the Capital Stock of the Company* (February 1833), 3, in Virginia State Archives; Joseph C. Cabell, *Address of Joseph C. Cabell to the Citizens of Richmond, On the 10th December 1834, on the Expediency of a Liberal Subscription to the Stock of the James River and Kanawha Company* (Richmond, VA: T.W. White,

1835), 13; Couper, *Crozet*, 56.

16. Lana Martindale, *Highways to Health and Pleasure: The Antebellum Turnpikes and Trade of the Mineral Springs in Greenbrier and Monroe Counties Virginia* (Pearisburg, VA: n.p., 1994), 9-11.

17. *Speech of Summers*, 41-42.

18. Clay to Calwell, February 24, 1829, in Mayo, "Henry Clay, Patron," *Virginia Magazine*, 306-7.

19. Robert Fleming Hunter, *The Turnpike Movement in Virginia, 1816-1860* (Ann Arbor, MI: UMI, 1957), 280-81, doctoral dissertation, Columbia University.

20. John Shawver and Others to A.A. Chapman, December 11, 1835, Alleghany County Legislative Petitions 1823-1839, A15, Folder A664, 10971, Virginia State Archives, Richmond.

21. Ibid.

22. Lewis H. Ripley, Jr., "Scott Tavern and the Scott-Price Family in Craig County, Virginia," *In and Around Craig County* (New Castle, VA: Craig County Historical Society, 1994), unnumbered; Shawver and Others to A.A. Chapman, December 11, 1835, Virginia State Archives.

23. A.J. Morrison, "Colonel Tatham and Other Virginia Engineers," in *William and Mary College Quarterly Historical Magazine*, 2, series 2 (1922), Kraus Reprint edition, New York, 1964, 81-82. Permission to cite and quote from *The William and Mary Quarterly* has been granted by the Earl Gregg Swem Library, College of William and Mary; A.J. Morrison, "The Virginia Literary and Evangelical Magazine, Richmond, Virginia, 1818-1828," in *William and Mary Quarterly*, 19 (1910-1911), Klaus Reprint edition, Millwood, NY, 1977, 271. Permission to cite and quote from *The William and Mary Quarterly* has been granted by the Earl Gregg Swem Library, College of William and Mary; William Maxwell, ed., "The

Shawnee Expedition in 1756," in *The Virginia Historical Register, and Literary Companion*, 5 (Spartanburg, SC: Reprint Company, 1973), 21; Alexander Scott Withers, *Chronicles of Border Warfare* (New York, NY: Arno Press & New York Times, 1971), IX; copy of letter from Hugh Paul Taylor to William Smith, August 26, 1828, in March 28, 1829, edition of the *Fincastle Mirror-Extra*. Found with Taylor's application for employment with the State of Virginia Board of Public Works. Box 49, 30030, Applications for Employment as Assistant Engineer; Hugh Paul Taylor Will, Dated December 1830, loose papers, Alleghany County Courthouse.

24. Morton, *Alleghany*, 59; Andrew Wilson testimony, April 6, 1850 in Booth v. Sweet Springs and Price's Mountain Turnpike Company, File 73, Alleghany County Courthouse; Swem, *Virginia State Bulletin-1916*, 1023.

25. *Early History of Alleghany County*, 8.

26. Pullen Sizer to author, August 21, 1995.

27. Swem, *Virginia State Bulletin-1916*, 1023-31.

28. *Early History of Alleghany County*, 6; *Twenty-Third Annual Report of the Board of Public Works, To the General Assembly of Virginia, with the Accompanying Documents, January 31, 1839.* (Richmond, VA: Shepherd & Colin, 1839), 222.

29. Ibid.

30. James Burk to J. Brown, Jr., December 8, 1838, in *Twenty-Third*, 430.

31. James Byrnside to Felix Hansford, June 7, 1850, Felix Hansford Papers, Folder 1850-1859, Box 1, A&M 1192, West Virginia and Regional History Collection, West Virginia University Libraries.

32. Statement of August 18, 1837 in Rich Patch Turnpike Company v. Mary Herbert's Executors.

33. Ibid.; Copy of legal statement, September 16, 1853, in Rich Patch Turnpike Company v. Mary Herbert's Executors; Petition to Honorable Edward B. Bailey in Rich Patch Turnpike Company v. Mary Herbert's Executors, July 12, 1853, Virginia State Archives.

34. Rich Patch Turnpike Company, Resolutions, Box 311, Board of Public Works Correspondence, Reports, etc., 1849-53, 2-3; Madison Hook to Board of Public Works, 19 October 1850, Box 311, Virginia State Archives.

35. RG29, T1132, Roll 5, U.S. Census (8th) Productions of Agriculture During the Year Ending June 1, 1860, Covington, Alleghany County, National Archives, 40.

36. Morton, *Alleghany*, 45.

37. Frank G. Leisure, *Geology of the Clifton Forge Iron District, Virginia, Bulletin of the Virginia Polytechnic Institute, Engineering Experiment Station Series No. 118*, Vol. L (May 1957), 80; *Early History of Alleghany County*, 14; Lester J. Cappon, "Lucy Selina's Charcoal Era," *Virginia Cavalcade* 7 (Autumn 1957), 31; Ibid., 36.

38. Leisure, *Geology*, 14.

39. Ibid., 81.

40. Steve Bostic, "Madison Bostic 1820-1892," *Monroe Watchman*, 19 August, 1993; *Early History of Alleghany County*, 11; "Old Tommie" Henning 1786-1875," *Journal of the Greenbrier Historical Society*, 109; Lois Lehner, *Lehner's Encyclopedia of U.S. Marks on Pottery, Porcelain & Clay* (Paducah, KY: Collector Books, 1988), 158; Kurt C. Russ, The Fincastle Pottery (44B0304): Salvage Excavations at a Nineteenth-Century Earthenware Kiln Located in Botetourt County, Virginia-Technical Report No. 3 (Richmond, VA: 1990).

41. J. Gray McAllister, *Sketch of Captain Thompson*

McAllister, Co. A, 27th Virginia Regiment (Petersburg, VA: Fenn & Owen, 1896), 12.

42. Ibid., 11-12; Ibid., 14.

43. *Proceedings of the Internal Improvement Convention, Held At The White Sulphur Springs, On The 24, 25 And 26 August, 1854; Together With A Paper Prepared By Mr. Fisk, Engineer Of The Covington And Ohio Railroad,-And Speeches Of Joseph Segar Of Elizabeth City, And Rich'd G. Morris, Of Richmond.* (Richmond, VA: Dispatch Journal, 1855), 3-4; Ibid., 9-12.

44. Ibid., 10-11; "Report of the Chief Engineer of the Covington & Ohio Railroad," in *Proceedings*, 1-3.

45. Henry T. Shanks, *The Secession Movement in Virginia, 1847-61* (New York, NY: AMS Press, 1971), 8-9.

46. Ripley, "Scott Tavern," *In and About Craig County*, unnumbered.

47. Pullen Sizer to author, August 21, 1995; Wood Map, Alleghany County Courthouse.

48. Pullen Sizer to author, August 21, 1995.

49. "Stringer's Tavern," WPA Inventory, Alleghany County, Virginia State Library.

50. Morton, *Alleghany*, 44; Perceval Reniers and Ashton Woodman Reniers, *The Midland Trail Tour in West Virginia: Being also An Account of the Old Stagecoach Days on the James River and Kanawha Turnpike* (New York, NY: Midland Publications Company, 1926), 8-9; Leila Blanche Bess, "Crow's Mill," University of Virginia Special Collections, Folklife Center, June 5, 1941, Potts Creek, VA, Acc. No. 1547, Box 6, Folder 1.

51. Reniers and Reniers, *The Midland Trail*, 8-9; Morton,

Alleghany, 92; *Early History of Alleghany County*, 8; "Crow's Tavern," in Gay Arritt, *Historical Sketches*, 93-94.

52. Haines, *Callaghan Mail*, 12-13.

53. "King's Tavern," in Arritt, *Sketches*, 91.

Chapter 5

1. Morton, *Alleghany*, 36; Morton, *Monroe*, 38.

2. Morton, *Monroe*, 386; RG15, Muster Rolls, August 31 & October 31, 1814, Box 271, National Archives; RG15, Paymaster's List, 4th Virginia Militia Regiment, Box 271, National Archives; John M. Hallahan, *The Battle of Craney Island*, 41; Ibid., 51-52.

3. RG15, Paymaster's List, Box 271, National Archives; Morton, *Monroe*, 371; RG15, James N. Linton Pension Records, National Archives.

4. *Biographical Directory of Congress*, 574; Rice, *Greenbrier*, 224.

5. Dunaway, *History of the James River & Kanawha*, 51-52; Leonard Jamison, "Another View: City's Namesake Gen. Leonard Covington," *Virginian Review*, 17 October 1994; Ibid., "Another View: General Leonard Covington," 14 November, 1994.

6. Donald R. Hickey, *The War of 1812-A Forgotten Conflict* (Chicago, IL: University of Illinois Press, 1989), 212.

7. RG15, Claim for Widow for Service Pension, Barbara Tingler, Certificate No. 30363, National Archives.

8. Morton, *Monroe*, 263-64.

9. Petition of James Burke, January 2, 1833, Alleghany County Legislative Petitions 1823-1839, A15, A660, 10201, Virginia State

Archives; Joseph Ervine Commissions, June 2, 1842, and December 29, 1845, property of Ginny McCue, San Jose, CA and John J. McCue, Leonardtown, MD.

    10. Brigade Returns, Doc. No. 1, Virginia General Assembly Senate Journals 1844, Film 332, 2, Virginia State Library.

    11. Muster Roll, Company K, U.S. Volunteers, 1847, Thornton T. Perry Miscellaneous Manuscripts Mss1 P4299g32, Virginia Historical Society, Richmond, VA; Zimmerman, "Sketches," 3 (1976), 28-29; RG15, Declaration of Survivor for Pension, Huram Baker Pension File, August 20, 1890, National Archives; RG 15, Claim of Soldier for Service Pension, Alexander M. Taylor Pension File, February 22, 1887, National Archives.

    12. Dorman, *Prestons of Smithfield*, 267; Zimmerman, "Sketches," 51-52.

    13. Keith Melder, *Hail to the Candidate-Presidential Campaigns from Banners to Broadcasts*(Washington, D.C.: Smithsonian Institution Press, 1992), 75.

Chapter 6

    1. Ralph Ketcham, *James Madison: A Biography* (Charlottesville, VA: University of Virginia, 1990), 57.

    2. Carl E. Burrows, *The History of Old Rehoboth Church From the Establishing of the First Class in 1784 To the Building of the Rehoboth Museum* (Charleston, WV: United Methodist Center, 1982), 3; Klaus Wust, *The Virginia Germans* (Charlottesville, VA: University Press of Virginia, 1969), 98.

    3. Ketcham, *Madison*, 57-58; Ibid., 163-65.

    4. Marcellus Zimmerman, "The Old Lewisburg Academy, by Marcellus Zimmerman," *Journal of the Greenbrier Historical Society* (3), 24; Ibid., 28; Rose W. Fry, *Recollections of the Rev. John*

McElhenney, D.D. (Richmond, VA: Whittet & Shepperson, 1893), 89; Ibid., 91.

5. *Journal and Proceedings of the Lewisburg Convention*, 15-16; Rice, *Greenbrier*, 217; Morton, *Alleghany*, 64.

6. Eugene C. Massie, "Journal of Captain Henry Massie," *Tyler's Quarterly Historical and Genealogical Magazine* 4 (October 1922), 77; Rice, *Greenbrier*, 217; George West Diehl, *Rev. Samuel Houston, V.D.M.* (Verona, VA: McClure Press, 1970), 81; Ibid., 87; Morton, *Monroe*, 227.

7. Howard McKnight Wilson, *The Lexington Presbytery Heritage: The Presbytery of Lexington and its Churches in the Synod of Virginia Presbyterian Church in the United States* (Verona, VA: McClure Press, 1971), 108.

8. Stoner, *Seed Bed*, 369.

9. Burrows, *History of Old Rehoboth*, 4.

10. Ibid., 20; Ibid., 5-7.

11. Wickline, "The Circuit Riders," 9; Burrows, *History of Old Rehoboth*, 9; Rice, *Greenbrier*, 217; Charles W. Turner, "California" Taylor of Rockbridge: "Bishop to the World," *Proceedings of the Rockbridge Historical Society* IX (Lexington, VA: 1982), 97; Morton, *Alleghany*, 211..

12. *Early History of Alleghany County*, 11; *Covington Virginian*, 29 October, 1965; John Clark Ridpath, ed., *William Taylor, Story of My Life, An Account of What I Have Thought and Said and Done in My Ministry of More Than Fifty-Three Years in Christian Lands and Among the Heathen. Written by Myself (New York, NY: Hunt & Eaton, 1896)*, 66.

13. *Covington* Virginian, 29 October 1965; *Early History of Alleghany County*, 12.

14. Roger E. Sappington, *The Brethren in Virginia: The History of the Church of the Brethren in Virginia* (Harrisonburg, VA: Committee for Brethren History in Virginia, 1973), 150.

15. Patricia Givens Johnson, "History of the Gravel Hill Church from the Old Record Book," from George Chapman Miller, *History and Membership of the Gravel Hill (Antioch) Christian Church Sinking Creek Valley Craig County, Virginia 1830-1871*, comp., 1974; J. William and Rebecca Austin, *Caldwell, Eakin, Lemon, Reid, and Related Families* (Roanoke, VA, 1982), 100.

16. Larry Adkins, *Rev. John Bragg (1815-c.1894) and the Baptist Church in Monroe County, West Virginia* (Beckley, WV: private printing, 1981), 4; Ibid., 6.

17. Reverend Victor C. LeClerq, CICM, *The Catholic Church in the Alleghany Highlands Around 1882* (n.p., 1983), 4-5.

18. *Early History of Alleghany County*, 2; LeClercq, *The Catholic Church*, 4-5.

19. Logan, *The Old Sweet*, 40; Lorenzo Dow, *Biography and Miscellany* (Norwich, Conn.: William Faulkner, 1834), 100.

20. Entry of April 7, 1805 and April 9, 1807 in Dow, *History of Cosmopolite*, 245-46; Ibid., 200.

Chapter 7

1. Haines, *Callaghan Mail*, 12-13.

2. Linkenhoker, *A History of Schooling*, 21; R. Duff Green, "A Governor of Virginia Who Never Ran For the Office," *Orange County Review*, 12 November 1992; Clyde R. Crosier, *The History of Education in Monroe County, West Virginia, 1796-1940*, Masters thesis, West Virginia University, 1940, 14-16.

3. Linkenhoker, *A History of Schooling*, 24-25.

4. Ibid., 30.

5. "Paint Bank hold savings full of memories," *New Castle Record*, 21 March, 1985, 4.

6. Rice, *Greenbrier*, 210; John F. Montgomery, "Lewisburg Known For Its Schools," *Journal of Greenbrier Historical Society*, 89; Zimmerman, "Old Lewisburg Academy," 25.

7. Ibid.

8. Ibid., 26.

9. Haines, *Callaghan Mail*, 12-13; Linkenhoker, *History of Schooling*, 31.

10. *Early History of Alleghany County*, 2; Morton, *Alleghany*, 66; Crosier, *History of Education in Monroe*, 14-15; Stoner, *Seed Bed*, 484.

11. Ibid.

12. Schoolmaster's Reports of Pupils and Attendance, Literary Schools, Monroe County, WV, T.W. Bellinger, Proj. No. WVA 3-13A, Roll 6, 1826-1855, 3; Ibid., 10; Ibid., 13.

13. Ibid., 11-13.

Genealogies

1. *Arritt* family taken from Louise Perkins, family lineage study, 426-32.

2. *Baker* family taken from Morton, *Monroe*, 303; Perkins, family lineage study, 557.

3. *Bland* family taken from author's file; Morton, *Monroe*, 313.

4. *Booth* family taken from Works Progress Administration records, Booth-Givens Tavern, Virginia State Library.

5. *Bostic* family taken from author's file; Morton, *Monroe*, 314. Thanks to Stewart Bostic for his great knowledge of the Bostic family.

6. *Callaghan* family taken from Morton, *Alleghany*, 127; Linkenhoker, *A History of Schooling in Alleghany*, 11, 17-18.

7. *Cloyd* family taken from A.D. Cloyd, *Genealogy of the Cloyd, Basye and Tapp Families in America* (Columbus, OH: Champlin Press, 1912).

8. *Dew* family taken from Wilmer L. Kerns, *Historical Records of Old Frederick and Hampshire Counties, VA* (Bowie, MD: Heritage Books, Inc., 1992).

9. *Dunbar* family taken from Morton, *Monroe*, 335-36.

10. *Ervine* family taken from Morton, *Alleghany*, 129; Nora Bragg Martin.

11. *Fudge* family taken from Morton, *Alleghany*, 129; Ibid., 153.

12. *Hook* family taken from author's files; Morton, *Alleghany*, 130-31.

13. *Jarvis* family taken from author's files; Nora Bragg Martin Papers.

14. *King* family taken from Morton, *Alleghany*, 131.

15. *Lewis* family taken from Morton, *Monroe*, 370-71.

16. *Linton* family taken from Nora Bragg Martin.

17. *McAllister* family taken from Morton, *Alleghany*, 132; James Gray McAllister, *McAllister Family Records, Compiled for the Descendants of Abraham Addams McAllister and his Wife Julia Ellen (Stratton) McAllister, of Covington, Virginia* (Easton, PA: Press of the Chemical Publishing Co., 1912).

18. *Massie* family taken from Morton, *Alleghany*, 134; *Tyler's Quarterly*, October 1922.

19. *Pennell* family taken from Morton, *Alleghany*, 134.

20. *Persinger* family taken from Persinger chart, Covington, VA; Morton, *Alleghany*, 135.

21. *Rose* family taken from author's files; Christine Rose, Rose Family Association (San Jose, CA) research reports; Sylvia S. Echols; Nora Bragg Martin; Louise Collins Perkins.

22. *Skeen* family taken from Morton, *Alleghany*, 138; "Petition to the General Assembly from the Convention at Lewisburg, For the Completion of the James River and Kanawha Improvement," *Journal of the House of Delegates. Session 1844-45.*, Doc. 7, 3; "Covington Convention," *Journal of the House of Delegates. Sessions 1846-47.*, Doc. 20, 4.

23. *Stull* family taken from Morton, *Alleghany*, 138.

24. *Taylor* family taken from Morton, *Alleghany*, 138; Hugh Taylor Will, Alleghany Court Courthouse.

25. *Walker* family taken from Works Progress Administration, Henry Walker House, Virginia State Library.

26. *Wright* family taken from Morton, *Alleghany*, 213; Nora Martin.

Bibliographical Notes on Sources

The book is divided into subject groups in the antebellum period, which divides easily for bibliographic purposes. There was a great amount of background needed to introduce the various subjects. For good general background sources, Oren T. Morton's *History of Monroe County, West Virginia* and *A Centennial History of Alleghany County* and Otis K. Rice's *History of Greenbrier County* cover the various localities from it root formations. Robert Douthat Stoner's *A Seed Beed of the Republic* was instrumental in its historical perspectives on Fincastle and Botetourt County, which before 1851 enveloped Craig County, Virginia. The other subjects are grouped below.

The Springs

General information on life at the springs was varied and expansive. I narrowed much of it to the central point of Sweet Springs, located between the towns of Covington, Lewisburg, and Union. The secondary sources used here was Frances Logan's book *The Old Sweet*, Stan Cohen's excellent pictoral book *The Springs of the Virginias*, and Perceval Reniers' *The Springs of Virginia*. There are numerous other excellent other books on the Sweet as well.

Various primary travel and religious accounts allow readers a detailed view of life at the springs. The best source on the early pre-1812 period includes James McHenry's letters in Bernard C. Steiner's

The Life and Correspondence of James McHenry, John Howell Briggs' journal, recounted in the Virginia Historical Society's booklet *First Resorts-A Visit to Virginia's Springs*, and Frederick Newbraugh's edition of *The Life and Adventures of Robert Bailey*. Another good primary source is Dr. John J. Moorman's journal, reprinted by the Greenbrier Historical Society in 1980, and his 1851 book *A Guide to the Virginia Springs*. The former is an account of White Suphur Springs. Dr. Quintard Taylor's 1923 book, *White Sulphur Springs: A Brief History* covers that spring and surrounding resorts and taverns. Some insights on the Red Sweet Springs, now Sweet Chalybeate, is in 1969 book by Louise Rawl, *Traveling Heritage Road*.

Anne Royall

The accounts of Anne Royall and her relations with the local citizens near Peter's Mountain are retold in Bessie Rowland James' book *Anne Royall's USA*, the only account that references the case details on this aspect of her life. The testimony and affidavits on the contest of William Royall's will, or Roane v. Royall, is located at the Augusta County Courthouse in Staunton, Virginia. Information on the Lewis family was obtained from Morton's histories and 1904 printed genealogy in the short-lived *West Virginia Historical Magazine Quarterly*.

Temperance

A lot of literature exists on the subject of temperance in the state of Virginia, but very little remains of western Virginia. Instrumental history is conveyed in C.C. Pearson and J. Edwin Hendricks' 1967 book, *Liquor and Anti-Liquor in Virginia, 1619-1919*. A more localized perspective is offered in the *Virginia Magazine of History and Biography*'s "Antebellum Liquor Reform in Lexington, Virginia: The Story of a Small Southern Town," by Ellen Esslinger. The most valuable sources came from temperance groups, such as the Sons of Temperance, in pamphlets and journals. Duke University has the important surviving journal of the Sons of Temperance Covington Division, which detailed the celebrations and commitments the mountaineers faced from 1849 to 1852. Also used were the minutes of an 1852 Fincastle meeting of the Sons of Temperance and printed for the general public from the collections of the Virginia State Archives in Richmond.

Politics

Politics is covered widely in the previously-noted county histories by Morton and Rice, but spreads into some valuable primary sources. Perhaps most unique are the Virginia Legislative Petitions, which are assembled by county and held at the Virginia State Archives. Political party structure, including the vital rivalry between Jacksonian Democrats and Clay Whigs, are recounted in many sources. Primary sources included a complete 1851 governor's poll vote for the county of Monroe. Helpful in outlining western Virginia political issues are Kenneth W. Noe's *Southwest Virginia's Railroad* and Charles Henry Ambler's 1913 book, *Thomas Ritchie: A Study in Virginia Politics*. Some interesting local insights are given in Harold H. Haines book, *The Callaghan Mail*.

Businesses

The history of western Virginia internal improvements is found in books on its champions, such as William Couper's 1936 book, *Claudius Crozet: Soldier-Scholar-Educator-Engineer*. An excellent account on the James River canal project is found in Wayland Fuller Dunaway's book, *History of the James River and Kanawha Company*. Journals and proceedings of individual improvement meetings, such as 1831 Lewisburg meeting, can be found at the Virginia State Archives. An excellent account of antebellum roads is found in Lana Martindale's unpublished manuscript, *Highways to Health and Pleasure: The Antebellum Turnpikes and Trade of the Mineral Springs in Greenbrier and Monroe Counties Virginia*. Equally important is Robert Fleming Hunter's dissertation on *The Turnpike Movement in Virginia, 1816-1860*.

For references on taverns, I researched the Craig County Historical Society's *In and Around Craig County*, Morton's county histories, and Gay Arritt's *Historical Sketches* of Alleghany County. Works Progress Administration records were consulted.

For information on the early iron industry in the area, I consulted *Virginia Cavalcade*'s 1957 article, "Lucy Selina's Charcoal Era," by Lester Cappon and Frank G. Leisure's *Geology of the Clifton Forge Iron District*, a report from Virginia Polytechnic Institute.

Other businesses, such as milling, ceramics, and furniture, were found in small notations in many places. The *Monroe Watchman* named several artisans. The *Journal of the Greenbrier Historical Society* also covers Lewisburg innovators.

Military Events

Generally three topics are covered: the War of 1812, the militia, and the Mexican War. The best primary source is pension records located in the National Archives. Several pension records of area veterans were consulted for both wars. Of regional interest is Leonard Jamison's fascinating articles on the founding of Covington in his column in the *Virginian Review*. For the War of 1812, John M. Hallahan's work, *The Battle of Craney Island: A Matter of Credit*, is a good reference work for Virginia activities.

Religion

Accounts by itinerants and denominational historians are among the most detailed records for the entire period. Aside from county histories, denominational accounts provided valuable information on day-to-day living. Certain works, like Reverend Carl E. Burrows' *The*

History of Old Rehoboth Church, recounted the beginning of Methodism in the area. Accounts by itinerant ministers, such as Lorenzo Dow and William Taylor, were helpful. Dwight Wickline's column in the *Monroe Watchman* on "The Circuit Riders" detailed the activities of local itinerant personalities. Presbyterian accounts were plentiful. *The Journal of the Greenbrier Historical Society* published journalist Marcellus Zimmerman's article on the Lewisburg Academy. George West Diehl's *Rev. Samuel Houston, V.D.M.* and Howard McKnight Wilson's *The Lexington Presbytery Heritage* were excellent sources. Additional material can be found in James Banks' thorough book *100 Years From Good Hope*. For information on Catholic activities, I consulted Reverend Victor C. LeClerq's *The Catholic Church in the Alleghany Highlands Around 1882*. A good local early Baptist account is Patricia Givens Johnson's "History of the Gravel Hill Church from the Old Record Book," from George Chapman Miller's *History and Membership of the Gravel Hill (Antioch) Christian Church*. There is material on Alexander Campbell's fundamental faith in the area in Roger E. Sappington's *The Brethren in Virginia*.

Education

The early schooling of the region can be studied in several educational accounts, such as Clyde Crosier's 1940 thesis from West Virginia University, *The History of Education in Monroe County, West Virginia, 1796-1940* and Paul Douglas Linkenhoker's dissertation from Virginia Tech, *A History of Schooling in Alleghany County, Clifton*

Forge, and Covington, Virginia. Some lists of literary schools are found at the Virginia State Archives.

Index

1st Regiment, Virginia Volunteers..................................... 78
108th Virginia Militia...76-77
111th Virginia Militia... 77
128th Virginia Militia...76-77
4th Virginia Militia...8, 74-75
79th Virginia Militia.. 75
Abingdon Banner.. 41
Adams, Asenith... 40
Albemarle County, Virginia... 77
Alderson, Joseph.. 23, 24
Alexander, Andrew... 51, 53
Alleghany County, Virginia..6, 7, 8
    27, 28, 29, 31, 33, 37, 43, 44, 45, 46, 47, 48, 49, 54
    59, 65, 67, 68, 71, 76, 77, 79, 80, 86, 89, 90
American Party...42
Anders, John...23
Andrews, Colonel...78
Aritt, Michael...18, 47
Armontrout, George.. 72
Armontrout, John.. 72
Arritt, John.. 47
Arthur, William... 38
Asbury, Francis..7, 11
    82-83

Bailey, Robert..13
Baker, Hiram..29, 77
        S.J... 29
Ball, Reuben.. 77
Baltimore and Ohio Railroad.. 54
Baltimore Conference, Methodist Church.............................83
Baptist.. 7, 28, 80
        85-86, 87, 89
Barber's Creek...13
Barbour, James..88
Bath County, Virginia..49
Battle of King's Mountain..74
Battle of New Orleans... 76
Battle of Point Pleasant..74
Battle of Vera Cruz..77-78
Baxter, Sidney...38
Bean, James F..91, 92
Bedford, Virginia..59
Beirne, Andrew.. 19, 22, 72
        75, 81
        Oliver...22, 24, 60
Benson, Ervin...16
Bess, Blanche...71
Beyer, Edward.. 24-25
Bias..17
Bishop, William..29

Black, Sam...........83
Blue Spring Run...........53
Blue Sulphur Springs...........56
Booth, William...........23, 26, 31
    44, 49, 58-59
Booth Tavern...........44, 70-71
Bostic, James...........39
    William...........67
Botetourt Central Democratic Committee...........36
Botetourt County, Virginia...........7, 8, 9
    13, 33, 43, 74, 76
Botts, John Minor...........40, 69
Boye Map...........53, 55
Breckinridge, James...........51
Brennemer, John...........82
Brethren, Church of the...........84, 85
Briggs, John Howell...........12-13
Brillhart, Reverend...........84
Brown, John...........62
Brown, Jr., John...........12
Bruffy, George W...........38
Buckingham County, Virginia...........74
Bullard, Chester...........85
Burk, James...........62, 63
Burwell, Thomas N...........36
Butler, Mary...........18, 19

Byrnside, James..63
Cabell, Joseph..55
Cadle, Jackson...67
Caldwell's Mountain...91
Cale, Chapman...91
Calhoun, John C..3, 33, 41
Callaghan, Charles...67
    Dennis...6, 21, 46
    50-51, 71, 72, 88
    John...48
    Oliver...36, 46, 47
    48
    William...47, 48, 88
Callaghans, Virginia....................................35, 47, 48
    60, 88
Calwell, J. Bowyer..46
    James..22, 34-35
    51, 67
    James H...77-78
Campbell, Alexander..85
    Calvin..38
    Clemons...38
Campbellites...85
Caperton, Allen Taylor..................................22, 24, 35
    37, 41, 69
    Hugh..22, 34

        35-36, 41

    Sarah......41

Carpenter, George W......91

    James......38

    Joseph......83

    Samuel......77

Carper, Benjamin......36

Carson, Elizabeth......20

    George......20

    James......23, 64

    William......64

Carter, John......29

Caruthers, Isaac......16-17

    William......51

Cary, Cyrus......47

Catholic Church......80, 86

Chapman, Augustus A......49

Charlottesville, Virginia......55

Church of St. John the Baptist......86

Clark, George Rogers......74

    Samuel......83

Clay, Henry......3, 16, 32-36
    41, 42, 46-47, 57-58, 68

Clifton Forge, Virginia......66

Clinton, DeWitt......54

Cokesbury Church......84

Cook, William..38-39
Cornstalk..3, 74
Cornwell, William...75
Counts, Charles..38
Covington, Gen. Leonard..75-76
Covington & Ohio Railroad..68, 69
Covington, Virginia..4-7, 27, 28, 29
    30, 43, 45, 47-48, 54, 55, 56, 57, 59, 61
    62, 63, 66, 68, 70, 72, 75, 82, 84
Covington Times..46
Craft, George W..77
Craig County, Virginia..31, 33, 43
    44, 48, 85
Craig's Creek..33
Craney Island, Virginia..74-75
Crosier, Martha..91
Crow, John..6, 68, 71-72
    76-77
Crozet, Claudius...55
Crutchfield, Francis...88
Culpeper County, Virginia...80
Cumberland County, Virginia...20
Cumberland, Maryland..52
Damron, Andrew..29, 31, 90
    Henry C...91
    Joseph..90

Daniel, Peter..89
Davidson, Andrew B..82
Deeds, Joseph..23
Democratic Party...32, 33, 36-
    37, 41, 42
Dew, Achilles...64
Dew's Chapel...83
Dinwiddie County, Virginia..12
Dodd, John..23
Dolly Ann Furnace..66
Donelson, Andrew Jackson..42
Dow, Lorenzo..7, 15, 86-87
Dunbar, John.. 38
    John A..40
    Margaret..40
    Matthew..2, 20-21
    Robert..38, 40
    Robert H..38
    William..38-40
Duncan, Landon...85
Dunlap Creek.. 4-5, 45, 62
    66, 75, 76
Dunsmore, Joseph...75
    William..75
Echols, John..22, 24
Episcopal Church.. 80, 81, 87

Erie Canal..54
Erskine, Henry...34, 78
    Jane..41
    William...16
Ervine, Joseph..65, 76, 77
    Sally..40
Falling Springs Presbyterian Church........................82
Falling Springs Valley...82
Farmer, C.E..29
Farmville, Virginia..59
Few, Samuel..29, 31
Fillmore, Millard...16
Fincastle, Virginia...7, 19, 31
    36, 68, 78, 87
Fincastle Democrat...46
Fincastle Mirror...46-47, 59
Flournoy, Thomas S..42
Floyd, John...21-22
    Lettie...21
Fontville...9
Fridley, Charles..30
Fry, Rose..81
Fudge, Andrew...46, 69
    Conrad..82
Fulton, George Newman....................................67-68
Gap Mills, Virginia (now WV).....................20, 38, 39

75, 81
Gatewood, Samuel..64
Giles County, Virginia...43, 85, 91
Gill, John...27
Givens, David..26, 37
Goode, John..33
Graham family...66
Gravel Hill Church..85
Greenbrier Association..85
Greenbrier County, Virginia (now WV).......................7, 24, 28
    33, 34, 41, 42, 55, 59, 74, 75, 77, 81, 85, 89
Greenwood, Henry..27
Hamilton, Andrew...46
Hansford, Felix G...63
Harrison, William Henry...78-79
Hawkins, Wellington..91
Haynes, William...81
Henning, Thomas..67
Herbert, Mary...64
    William..18
Hill, Clifton...48
Holloway, John..47
    Lewis...46
    William..47
Hook, Madison..44, 65
    Stephen..48, 63, 64

Houston, Sam...6
    Samuel..82
    Samuel R...8, 82
Howard's Creek...62
Hughart, William...85
Humphries, Jesse.......................................27, 66
    William..23
Hutchinson, Beniah..46
    George W..23
    John..9, 23-24
Indian Creek Church................................28, 85-86
Irvine, John..6, 66
Jackson, Andrew....................................3, 33, 36
    58
Jackson River...5, 75
James River & Kanawha Canal...................5, 33, 52
    55, 70, 75
James River & Kanawha Company..............5, 35, 53
    54, 56, 59, 62
Jamison, George......................................65, 84
Jarvis, Daniel..75
    Field..21, 39-40
    Field A..23, 38, 39
        40
    Field W...38, 40
    John...23, 38, 39

    40
- Mary Ann...40
- Nancy..40
- Susannah...40
- William Fletcher..38, 40

Jefferson, Thomas...6, 15, 16, 36, 53
Johnson, Jake...84
- Joseph...37, 40
- William..53

Jordan, Edwin...63, 64, 67
- John...6, 66-67

Jordan Mines..6, 66
Kanawha County, Virginia (now WV)..........................9, 21
Keenan, Edward..80
Keyser, Fleming...71
King, Charles..90
- John..63, 65

Lafayette, Marquis de..16
Lane, William..85
Lanius, John..48
Lawhorn..91
LeClercq, Victor..86
Lewis, Andrew..3
- Charles..3
- John...2, 3, 4, 15

       18-21, 25
    Susan Preston..82
    William.. 3, 4, 9, 15
       22, 51
    William Lynn..16, 21, 22
Lewis family...1, 3, 21
   22, 24, 25
Lewisburg, Virginia (now WV)............................. 3, 4, 9, 28
   33, 36, 50, 51, 52, 55, 56, 59, 75, 78, 81, 83, 89
Lexington, Virginia..28, 72, 81
Lexington & Covington Turnpike Company......................56, 72
Linton, Elizabeth..23
    George A..40
    James..2
    James N.. 18, 22, 75
    John..23, 40
Literary Fund... 88, 89, 90
       92
Logan, Frances..16
Longdale, Virginia...67, 72, 86
Lucy Selina Furnace...66
Lynchburg, Virginia..54, 59
Madison, Bishop James.................................... 11, 13, 14
   15, 86
    James...6, 16, 80-81
Mallow, George..27

Mann, John McD..90
Marshall, John..51
Massie, Henry..82
Mastin, John..45
Matheny, George..29
Mathews, James W...75
McAllister, Thompson...29, 31, 68-69
McDonald, Angus...41
McDowell, James...36, 51, 77
McElhenney, John..8, 20, 28
    81-82, 89-90
McHenry, James...4, 10-13
McNutt, John...91
Merriweather, W.D..53
Merry, James..4-5, 27
Methodist Church..7, 11, 15
    80, 82-85, 87
Minor, Dabney..12
Monroe County, Virginia (now WV).........................8, 9, 15
    23, 28, 34, 37, 39, 41, 42, 43, 44, 47, 48, 49, 55
    63, 67, 72, 74, 75, 76, 77, 79, 81, 86, 91
Montgomery County, Virginia..............................9, 41, 85
Montgomery Presbytery..82
Moomaw, B.F...84
Moorman, John...13-14, 24
    34-35

Morton, Oren 48
Mount Carmen 86
Mountain House Tavern 60, 70-71
Mountain Lake and Salt Sulphur Springs Turnpike
   Company 56
Neel, Daniel 39
      Thomas W 38
      William 38, 39
New Castle, Virginia 41, 82, 85
Nickell, Andrew 8, 74, 75
Nininger, Peter 84
Noe, Kenneth W 41, 42
Norfolk, Virginia 74, 76
Orange, Virginia 12
Paint Bank, Virginia 38, 89
Parker, James 39
Pattison 27
Patton, John 75
      William 38
Paxton, James 36
Pence, George 5
Pencil, Mark 17
Pennell (Pinnell), Joseph 7, 84
      Mrs 84
Persinger, John 53, 66
      Jacob 27

Moses..53
Peter's Mountain... 2, 3, 6, 38
    44
Peterstown...86
Peyton, Charles L..36
Pierce, Franklin..16
Pinnell's Chapel...84
Pitzer, John...4, 5, 29
    31, 76
Polk, James..42
Potts Creek/Valley.......................................1, 2, 3, 5
    6, 7, 21, 22, 24, 26, 28, 30, 38, 43, 45, 47, 53, 65
    66, 68, 75, 76, 82, 83, 84, 91
Potts Mountain..39, 43
    60, 70
Presbyterian Church......................................7, 21, 28
    38, 56, 80, 81, 82, 87, 89
Preston, David R..81
    James Francis...41, 78
    William..34, 41
Price, Jacob..58, 70
    Samuel..69
Printz, William...29
Pritt, Elijah..75
    Robert..75
Pugh, James F..92

Randolph, Thomas Mann..53-54
Rayhill, Alexander...23, 90
    Matthew..75
Red Sweet Springs... 14, 16, 17
Rehoboth Church.. 11, 80, 82
    83
Republican Party...42
Reynolds, Johnson..46
    Lewis S...91
Rich Patch.. 27, 30, 44
    63-65, 66, 82, 84
Rich Patch Turnpike Company.............................56, 61, 63-65
Richmond, Virginia.. 37, 43, 56
    63, 67, 69, 74
Ritchie, Thomas..41
Rives, William Cabell..33, 69
Roane, Elizabeth...18
    James...18
    William...19
Roaring Run..64, 66
Robinson, John...29
    Samuel C...63
Rockbridge County, Virginia...66
Rocky Point..20
Rogers, James..29
    W.B...67

Rose, Henry B. 30
Rosenham, Leo. 29
Rowan, William. 38
Royall, Anne. 1, 2-3, 6
    18-21
    William. 1, 2, 17-21
Rusk, Samuel. 38
Salem & New Castle Turnpike Company. 61
Salt Sulphur Springs. 16, 17, 41
Sawyers, Sampson. 90
Scott, Mrs. 70
    William. 29, 70
Scott's Tavern. 70
Segar, Joseph. 69
Shawver, Christopher. 2
    Elizabeth. 18
    Jacob. 8, 21
    John. 2, 58
    Margaret. 44
Shawver Tavern. 6, 70
Shirkey, Carleton. 63
Shoaf's Chapel. 84
Singleton, Colonel. 35
    Mrs. 35
Sinking Creek. 85
Sinks Grove Church. 86

Sizer, Pullen..70
Skeen, Robert...45
Smith, Ballard..34, 52
      Henry..90
      James..21
      Thomas..64
      William...59
Snake Run..4, 11, 53, 64
Sons of Temperance.......................................7, 28-31, 32
Staunton, Virginia.....................................1, 18, 35, 51, 58
Steele, Campbell..39
      George..38
Stevenson, Andrew..21, 35, 69
Stillings, Thomas..29
Stoner, Robert Douthat..13
Stringer, John..6, 71
      William R..91
Stull, Isaac...90
Sugar Bottom Schoolhouse..44
Summers, George W.................................37, 39, 40, 55, 57
Sweet Springs..................................1, 3, 4, 6, 9, 10, 11, 12, 13, 15, 16, 17, 19, 20, 21, 22, 23, 24, 25, 38,

    39, 43, 44, 53, 60, 70, 71, 82, 86

Sweet Springs & Fincastle Turnpike...................................26, 44

Sweet Springs & Price's Mountain Turnpike..................38, 58, 60
    61

Sweet Springs & Salt Sulphur Springs Company.......................61

Sweet Springs Company...17, 24, 25

Tarleton, Banistre...1

Taylor, Hugh Paul... 4, 27, 52-54
    59-60, 84

    William...83-84

    Zachary...40, 77

Terrill, William...49, 54

Thomas, Joseph..85

Thompson, John W...36

    Larkin...77

Thomson, Jane..21

Tingler, Jacob..76

Tunnell, John...83

Tyler, John..5, 88, 89

Tyree, John..27

Union, Virginia (now WV)..9, 19, 22
    24, 25, 28, 35, 39, 43, 51, 67, 76, 81, 82

Van Buren, Martin...41, 72

Vawter, James..44

Vines, Silas..29

Virginia Constitutional Convention 1829-30.........................32

Virginia Department (Bureau) of Public Works............51, 60
Walker, Henry A..91
       Martha A..92
Walker family..70
Walters, John...86
Walton, Harry...5
Warm Springs..35, 50
Warren, James..90
Washington, George...6, 47
Washington, D.C..13, 43
Watson, John...92
Westmoreland County, Virginia..77
Whig Party...32, 33, 34
    36, 37, 38, 40, 41, 42, 47, 68
White, Hugh Lawson..33, 34
White & Salt Sulphur Turnpike Company............................56
White Sulphur Springs, Virginia (now WV).............13-14, 16
    22, 24, 34, 35, 51, 67, 69, 70, 71, 77
Wickline, Jacob..37
       Jake..84
Wiley, Ferdinand..48
       Francis A..23
       James..2, 18, 19
    20, 44
       John S...23
Wilson, Andrew..23, 60

George W..36
Wise, Henry..42, 70
Wiseman..91
Withrow, William E.......................................89
Wolf, John...23
Wolf family..53
Wolfe's Chapel...84
Woltz, Jacob..36
Wood, John..53
Woodville, James...21
      Mary Sophia...............................21
Worsham, Daniel..39
Wright, James..83
      Peter..82
Wylie, Robert...75
      Thomas...75
Wythe County, Virginia...............................66, 85
Younger, John W..48

www.ingramcontent.com/pod-product-compliance
Lightning Source LLC
Chambersburg PA
CBHW060520090426
42735CB00011B/2306